ANYBODY GOT A CLUE ABOUT GUYS?

ANYBODY GOT A CLUE ABOUT GUYS?

A Young Woman's Guide to Healthy Relationships

Susie Shellenberger

Servant Publications
Ann Arbor, Michigan

Vine Books is an imprint of Servant Publications especially designed to serve
evangelical Christians.

Scripture references were taken from *The Living Bible* (LB), © 1971 by Tyndale
House Publishers, Wheaton, Illinois 60187. All rights reserved.

GUYS: How do You Know if You Like the Right One? by Susie Shellenberger first
appeared in the June 1995 issue of *Brio*.

Living in Another World by Susie Shellenberger first appeared in the June 1994
issue of *Brio*.

The names and pictures of those whose full names appear in this book are real and
have been used by permission. Where first names only have been used, the name
has been changed to protect the privacy of those in the story.

Thanks to Michael Ross, editor of *Breakaway* magazine, for his contribution in the
chapter on singleness.

Thanks to the girls who sent questions to *Brio* magazine that were used for this
book.

Thanks to *Brio* magazine, published by Focus on the Family, for reprint of the Guy
Talk sections.

Thanks to Bob Smithouser and the Youth Culture staff at Focus on the Family for the
information on the media found in chapter thirteen.

Published in association with Alive Communications, Inc., 1465 Kelly Johnson Blvd.,
Suite 320, Colorado Springs, CO 80920.

Published by Servant Publications
P.O. Box 8617
Ann Arbor, Michigan 48107

Cover design by Multnomah Graphics, Portland, Oregon
Cover photos:Craig Strong Photography
Interior photo of Cindy Morgan: Michael Haber. Used by permission.

95 96 97 98 99 10 9 8 7 6 5 4 3 2 1

Printed in the United States of America
ISBN 0-89283-911-2

Library of Congress Cataloging-in-Publication Data

Shellenberger, Susie.
    Anybody got a clue about guys? : a young woman's guide to healthy
relationships / Susie Shellenberger.
       p.   cm.
    Summary: Offers advice with a Christian perspective on the psychological,
social, and physical aspects of relationships between teenagers.
    ISBN 0-89283-911-2
    1. Sex—Religious aspects—Christianity—Juvenile literature. 2.
Interpersonal relations—Religious aspects—Christianity—Juvenile literature. 3.
Dating (Social customs)—Religious aspects—Christianity—Juvenile literature.
4. Sexual ethics for teenagers. 5. Teenage girls—Conduct of life. 6. Teenage
girls—Religious life. [1. Interpersonal relationships. 2. Sexual ethics. 3. Dating
(Social customs) 4. Christian life.] I. Title.
BT708.S525 1995
248.8'33—dc20
                                       95-31926
                                        CIP AC

DEDICATION

To Mallory Bergland. May all your relationships with guys be fun, healthy, and godly.

Love, Aunt Susie

YOUR GUIDE TO WHAT'S INSIDE

Part 5 Creating Positive Dating Memories

So, You Want to Know More about Guys...

HI, I'm Susie! If there's one thing I'm crazy about it's teens. I love 'em. That's why I'm committed to helping them understand themselves, God's plan, and the opposite sex just a little better. And the opposite sex is what this book is all about.

I think I'm pretty lucky, because I believe I have the best job in the whole world. I get to create a fun, colorful magazine for teen girls—just like you—every month. It gives me an exciting opportunity to be involved in a special way in their lives.

Being a magazine editor gives me a chance to hear from a lot of girls—I get about a thousand letters a month addressed to *Brio* magazine. Most of those letters are filled with questions about the opposite sex. And since I couldn't answer all the mail, I decided to write this book. The following pages are filled with all the things teen girls want to know about guys!

I hope you'll enjoy the stuff I'm passing on to you. But more important, I hope you don't keep it to yourself. Share it with your friends. Talk about it with your mom and dad. And send me your thoughts. I'd love to hear from you!

Your Friend,

Susie

1143 Highland Dr., Suite E
Ann Arbor, MI 48108

PART 1
Foundations for Great Friendships

Why do guys always want a female lab partner in biology class?

"The biology room usually has this weird odor. So guys want a female lab partner who'll always look and smell good."

Jay DeMarcus, East to West

Why do so many guys have sloppy handwriting?

"We jot down what we have to and get it over with. Guys are usually in a hurry. Girls like to write with bubbly letters or play with what they're writing. They generally take time to write just the right stuff. They want it not only to *sound* good but to *look* good as well."

Chris Kendall, 15

Why do guys play with their food and mix it together in the school cafeteria?

"Because we like to show off. If no one was watching, we probably wouldn't do it. Once in a while, someone will dare you to EAT what everyone has mixed up, and to actually swallow it makes you feel cool."

Adam, 12

Chapter One

YOUR BEST FRIEND

Before the opposite sex will start liking you, you have to like yourself. Here's why:

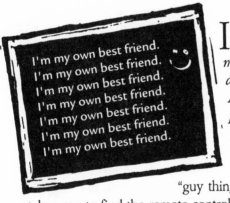

I'm my own best friend.
I'm my own best friend.
I'm my own best friend.
I'm my own best friend.
I'm my own best friend.
I'm my own best friend.
I'm my own best friend.

I know what you're thinking: *Hurry! Give me some quick answers about the male species. After all, that's why I picked up this book. So let's get moving!*

Be patient! I'll bet we'll be into the "guy thing" in less time than it takes you to find the remote control to the TV. But before we can talk woman to woman about GUYS, we need to chit-chat about the girl who's reading these words right *now*. (Yep, that's YOU!)

Ever heard the expression "Love thy neighbor as thyself"? Those were words from Jesus himself, but have you ever thought about what they really mean? There's a lot of wisdom behind those words. They tell you that before you can truly accept those around you, you first have to accept *yourself*. Well, the same holds true with those sometimes hard-to-understand creatures called *guys*. They won't even be *interested* in you until *you* become interested in *yourself*.

Stick with me. It'll all make sense when you read about a young woman who understood what it took to make herself interesting to other people.

ERIN'S BEST FRIEND

Erin always seemed so confident around guys. She wasn't knock-out gorgeous or anything like that. But there was something about her that made her feel completely comfortable around guys. She talked with ease to the football and basketball players, guys in the band, and the new guys in her school.

And how did the guys respond to Erin? They were always around her! Her yearbook was always the first to fill up with signatures. She never stood alone at her locker, and guys always headed to *her* table in the cafeteria during lunch time.

What was her secret? Why did all the guys seem so drawn to Erin? Well, Erin had a special "in" with her best friend. You see, if we have at least one person who really believes in us, affirms us and loves us, we can learn to be confident. Erin had a best friend who did just that. She was always there for Erin. She always listened to her, cried with her, and laughed with her.

Sound like a friend *you'd* like to have? You can! You see, Erin's best friend was none other than herself. Think about it: You can either be your own worst enemy... or you can be your own best friend!

Erin was smart enough to become her own best friend. She learned not just to *accept* herself, but to *like* herself. And that made all the difference in the world when she talked to others, including the guys!

THE LOYALTY QUOTIENT

How about you? Are you your own best friend? Or can you barely accept yourself? Maybe you don't even like yourself. Always remember that how you see yourself will affect how others see you.

To see where *you* fall in the "self's best friend" category, let's check your loyalty quotient. Grab a pencil and mark the responses to the following statements that are closest to what you would say in the same situation. (It's OK to write in this book, I promise.)

1. I just blew the pop history quiz Mrs. Bergland gave in fifth period. My response to myself:
   __ a. "How could I be so stupid? Now I'll never pass."
   __ b. "It was a tough quiz, and it was a total surprise. Next time, I'll be better prepared."

2. I just found out I didn't make the drill team. My response to myself:
   __ a. "It was ridiculous of me to even dream of being on the drill team in the first place."
   __ b. "A lot of talented girls tried out. I'll work hard over the summer—maybe get some extra coaching—and try out again next year."

3. I make a quick trip to the bathroom between third and fourth period classes and notice that my hair has gone completely limp. My response to myself:
   __ a. "I look like such a dweeb! No wonder Brett never talks to me. I have the grossest hair."
   __ b. "Maybe I ought to play around with my hair tonight and try a few different things with it. Or maybe mom will let me make an appointment with a stylist. This is really good for a laugh!"

4. I'm wearing a dress to school and notice during lunchtime that I have a three-inch run between my knee and ankle. My response to myself:

___ a. "Something dumb like this ALWAYS happens when I try to dress up. I look so stupid! Maybe if I keep my head down, no one will notice."

___ b. "Wow! That's a pretty good racing stripe. I'll borrow some fingernail polish from Katie and make a joke out of it if anyone says anything."

5. I'm interested in getting to know Geoff better. We've been talking quite a bit for the past three days. Today, though, when I see him at school, he walks past me without saying a word. My response to myself:

___ a. "Uh oh. He hates me! I must have said something stupid yesterday. I'm so geeky!"

___ b. "I wonder if Geoff is going through a hard time. I think I'll jot him a quick note reminding him to have a great day."

SCORING

If you selected mostly B's for your responses, you're in the process of learning to like who you are. But if you marked a lot of A's, then you probably need to change the way you see yourself.

How others see you. The really catchy thing about all this is that however *you* feel about yourself will eventually be reflected in how *others* feel about you. So the bottom line is this: Want to be liked by both guys *and* gals. Then start liking yourself!

Learning to accept and feel good about who you are is really not that difficult. Here are four sure-fire ways to get headed in the right direction.

1. Glory in your gifts—Jot down all the things you do well *as well as* the things you're in the process of *learning* to do well. You're pretty good at horseback riding? Great! Write it down. You've been taking piano lessons? Excellent! Put it on the list. Be kind to yourself. Any talent, gift, or character quality you have can go on your list.

(If you're having trouble thinking of things you're good at, see if anything here will spark some of your own ideas about what you do well at: writing letters, cooking, cleaning the house, making friends, singing, making crafts, thinking up new ways to do things, entertaining friends in your home, taking really good notes in class, being punctual, playing sports, making new people feel accepted, being artistic, asking well-articulated questions, being poetic, organizing, teaching Sunday school, reading, retaining what you read.)

After you've listed what you do well, study your list for a few minutes. Then take time to realize that God is the one responsible for giving you the abilities and talents that you have. Take a few seconds right now to thank him for making you the way he did. (Either read this prayer to him, or write out your own prayer in the space provided.)

Dear Jesus,

I never realized that you created me with so much ability. I admit I've taken several things in my life for granted. Thanks so much for giving me the ability to do these things well. Please help me to become even better in these areas. Help me to feel good about the things you've gifted me in. I want to believe in myself and be the confident young lady you want me to be. Thanks, Jesus! Amen.

_____

_____

_____

_____

2. List your likes—Don't put that pen down! We're not finished. (You *can* go grab a diet cherry 7-Up, though, if you need a break.) Next, list all the things you like about yourself. (Again, if you're having trouble thinking of things, use this list to get started: I like my handwriting, my hair color, the way I tan in the summer, my spirit of adventure, my height, the way I walk, my determination, my spontaneity, my shoe size, my laugh, the fact that I'm a good listener, the way I take care of my pet, my availability to those around me.)

When you've finished your list of likes, give it a good read-through. You really have a LOT going for you, don't you? Wouldn't *you* love to be friends with someone who has all these great attributes? You can! But if you're not used to being positive with yourself, it will take conscious effort. Let's talk to the One who made you. After all, God is the one who can best transform negative thoughts into positive ones. That's one of his specialties!

(Again, you can either read this prayer to God or write out your own in the space provided.)

Dear Father,

I guess it's easier to think positively about myself when I'm staring at a list of things I like. I'm sorry that I tend to get down on myself so often. I realize that you made me in your image. What an honor! Teach me that you want me to feel good about who you've made me to be.

Help me not to focus so much on the things I don't do well. Instead, help me to zero in on all the positive stuff in my life. Teach me to change my thought patterns from negative to positive.

I realize that when that happens, it will affect how I see those around me... and even how THEY see ME! I want that positive change, Lord. Thanks so much for believing in me. Amen.

---

3. Perk up for positives—Talk to a few adults you trust (your parents, youth leader, Sunday school teacher, older cousin), and tell them you're trying to learn to like yourself better. Ask them to take the time to praise you for positive things they see in your life. *That's* certainly worth perking up for, isn't it? We ALL like to hear about our positive qualities, don't we?

If you feel comfortable doing this with your mom, it could become a really encouraging nighttime tradition for the two of you. Before you go to bed, spend some time affirming one another and praying together. You'll be amazed at the incredible difference a few weeks of verbal affirmation will make in how you view yourself (and your mom)!

4. Get it from God—Since God is the one who created you, it stands to reason that he knows you better than anyone else. But the *really exciting* thing is that even though he KNOWS you—inside and out, the good AND the bad—he also LOVES you more than anyone else!

Take advantage of God's love for you. If you're not already spending time with him every day—reading your Bible and talking with him (many people call this special time devotions)—then discipline yourself to begin now.

The better you get to know your Heavenly Father, the better you'll get to know yourself. Search for Scriptures that affirm how much God loves you. Jot them down, memorize them, hang them in your locker—saturate your mind with them. The more positive ammunition you store in your brain, the better view you'll have of yourself. And the faster you learn to like *you,* the faster you'll become your own best friend. The better you get to know your heavenly Father, the *better* you'll become your own best friend.

PEOPLE ALWAYS NOTICE

A confident person stands out in every crowd! That's why everyone was attracted to Erin. It wasn't her looks, her clothes, or her cologne. It was simply because she likes who she is. Therefore, she's assured and poised when she's around the opposite sex.

Not only are *guys* drawn to girls who feel good about themselves, but everyone notices a secure individual. You want to be that person? Then start now by becoming your own best friend!

Why is it hard for guys to reach out to new kids?

"It's all dependent on a guy's sense of security. Most guys create a situation in which they feel very comfortable (a circle of friends, a specific area of involvement), and they don't want to venture beyond that sense of security. This is why you don't see many guys reaching out or stretching themselves in that way."

Tom, 18

Why don't guys bring what they need to class?

"Because asking for a piece of paper or a pen gives us a reason to talk to the girls."

Mark Lowry, Christian comedian

Chapter Two
DADS, MOMS, AND DAUGHTERS

Believe it or not, they really DO go together!

I sn't it just like parents to show up now? Here we are, just getting into talking about how to relate to guys, then into the conversation comes dad and mom! It's not that you don't like including them in your life, but there are times when you'd just rather talk to someone else about things.

But your parents have much more to do with how you relate to the opposite sex than you might think. After all, your parents are the ones who had the biggest hand in making you the kind of person you are. So learning how to get along with and relate better to guys also means we get to take an exciting peek at what makes *you* tick. That's where your parents come in.

DADS AND DAUGHTERS

Your earthly father has a most special role in your life. Your dad is the one who can help you appreciate your femininity and be proud of your physical attractiveness. You can actually receive many cues from *him* about how to relate to the other guys in your life. If you have a healthy relationship with your father, chances are you'll establish healthy friendships with guys.

It's God's design that your dad is a healthy male role model for you. The qualities that you admire most in him are the same characteristics you'll wind up looking for in the guys you date.

Ideally, you're able to view your dad's relationship with your mom as a healthy male/female bond. You notice that he works hard to provide a home for her and the rest of your family, and that he takes great care to protect his loved ones.

If your parents have a good marriage, you'll also see that your dad assumes the role of leadership within your family. He doesn't act like a dictator and demand his own way, but he gently guides the family in the direction he believes God is leading him. These are all important things worth seeking out in your own relationships with the opposite sex.

A DATE WITH YOUR DAD

Again, a healthy relationship with your dad will help you develop solid friendships with guys. Why not set aside a specific night next week to go on a date with your dad. He'll love it!

Ask your father ahead of time if the two of you can spend an evening together. It might be at his favorite restaurant or a picnic in the park. It doesn't have to be expensive—just planned ahead of time. If he's short on time next week, ask if you can grill a couple of hot dogs for him in the backyard for your time together. The goal here is simply to spend some uninterrupted time together. Make it an activity that will allow the two of you to really talk with one another.

Ask him what will help you develop good, healthy relationships with guys. Here is a list of good questions to start with:

- ☞ What are the qualities in Mom that you admire?
- ☞ Do you see any of those qualities in me?
- ☞ What would other guys admire about me?
- ☞ How can I be friendly but not flirty with guys?
- ☞ What are the most important things you think I should look for in my relationships with guys?
- ☞ What are the top three reasons why you and Mom have a good relationship?
- ☞ What do I need to watch out for when going out with guys?
- ☞ What do you perceive are my areas of vulnerability?
- ☞ How can I help a guy feel confident about himself?
- ☞ (Add a few questions of your own.)

WHAT TO WATCH OUT FOR

If your father isn't a healthy role model, or if you don't have a father in your home, don't be discouraged. You can still establish terrific relationships with guys!

Begin asking now that God bring a godly male adult into your life who can give you some affirmation and guidance.

This might be your youth pastor, a teacher, or your pastor.

I need to stop and give you a word of warning here. I wish I didn't have to add this, but I need to be as honest and up-front with you as I can. You need to know that just because someone is an adult—or even in a respected position—it doesn't always mean that the person is trustworthy. We've all heard and read about situations in which adults have taken advantage of vulnerable teen girls.

Before you accept an adult male as a role model, look for the answers to these questions:

- ☞ Is he a Christian?
- ☞ What kind of reputation does he have?
- ☞ Have you ever known him to be in a compromising situation?
- ☞ Is he a man of integrity?
- ☞ How does he act around other teens?
- ☞ What specifically makes you think he might be a good role model for you?
- ☞ Can you trust him?
- ☞ What do your parents think of him?
- ☞ What do other adults think of him?

If there are even *two* of the above questions that you can't answer positively about your potential role model, then you need to look for someone else.

LOOKING IN THE WRONG PLACES

Girls who don't have a healthy relationship with their dads sometimes tend to look for love in the wrong places and in the wrong ways.

How about you? If you don't have a solid relationship with your dad, mark the following statements that apply to you:

__ I crave attention from guys.

__ I'm a big flirt.

__ I'll do just about anything to get a guy to notice me.

__ I chase guys.

__ I often call guys and write them notes.

__ I kiss a lot of guys.

__ I touch guys a lot.

__ When on a date, it's rare that I'm the one who backs off when things get physical.

__ When on a date, I often initiate physical contact.

__ If a guy *didn't* kiss me, I'd assume something was wrong.

If you marked two or more of the above statements, chances are that you're looking for love but accepting physical involvement as a substitute.

Sex is not love, and it never will be. It's normal to want attention from a male. God created that desire within all women. But when a girl doesn't receive love and affection from her father, she'll often try to get it from other men, not realizing that no guy can offer her what a father should be demonstrating.

Again, you may or may not fall into this category. But if you *don't* have a solid relationship with your dad, be sure to guard yourself in these areas of vulnerability, because it *will* affect how to relate to the opposite sex.

MOMS AND DAUGHTERS

Just as your father has a special role in your life, your mother also plays an important role.

Your mom is the very source of your female identity. Since you and your mom are both females—and identical on the inside—you share a bond that's found only in a mother/daughter relationship.

If you have a close relationship with your mother, then you probably feel good about yourself and your developing body. This in turn will help you feel confident as you establish relationships with guys.

One of the most confusing and frustrating times for a young girl is when her body begins to develop as she matures. It's natural to feel self-conscious about your budding growth and to wonder if what's happening is really normal.

Girls can feel frustrated or embarrassed when they start developing physically before any of their friends. These girls sometimes have to deal with being the only ones in their class who have started having their period or have begun developing breasts. Other girls are made fun of because they *haven't* developed breasts or started their menstrual cycle yet. The showers and locker rooms can be an especially frightening place to discover how "ahead" or "behind" schedule you are.

The truth is, no matter *when* you begin your physical development, you're normal—as in right on schedule! Doctors say that normal is anywhere between the ages of nine and seventeen years of age.

CHITCHAT WITH MOM

During this awkward stage of life, it's often much easier to look at all the things you see *wrong* with your body than to look at everything that's going *right*. This is where a healthy relationship with your mom can make all the difference in the world.

Ask your mom if the two of you can have a special night together next week, similar to the evening you spent with your dad. Asking her the following questions will help you feel good about yourself and will aid in establishing quality relationships with guys. (And if your mom isn't accessible, ask God to provide an adult woman you *can* talk with. But be sure you go through the same questions listed for talking with an adult male role model. You want a woman you can trust!)

☞ How do I know how to find the right bra size for me?

☞ What's the advantage of tampons versus pads?

☞ What do you see in me that guys will find attractive?

☞ What top things initially attracted you to Dad?

☞ Have those things changed during the years? Do you find yourself attracted to him now for different reasons?

☞ How can I make sure I don't date just to be dating?

☞ What are some specific ways I can really get to know a guy before going out with him?

☞ How can I tell the difference between a guy who really cares about me and a guy who just wants to date?

☞ What do you perceive are my areas of vulnerability?

☞ How can I be a girl all the guys feel good about being around?

☞ What do you perceive to be my strengths?

☞ (Add a few questions of your own.)

TREASURE YOUR PARENTS

Since you're reading this book, it's obvious that you really care about how you relate to the opposite sex. You want to find out what makes guys tick, how to become friends with them, and how to feel good about yourself when you're around them.

You begin to learn this as you learn to value your parents. Dad and mom play a major role in how you relate to guys.

Use your parents as resources in this area. Ask them a million questions, seek their advice, and don't hesitate to share your concerns with them. You'll benefit from the wisdom they have to offer, and they'll love helping you discover the fun of developing terrific relationships.

What do you think about girls who make the first move?

"That was always a turnoff to me. I didn't like a girl who was so anxious to have a relationship or go out on a date that she would make the first move. *I* always wanted to ask the questions and approach her first."

Andy Chrisman, 4HIM

Why do a lot of guys chew tobacco?

"We see so many sports celebs doing it that it's easy to believe it makes you look cool. Lots of guys use it as sort of a tension reliever. Personally, I think it's stupid... something *I'd* never do."

Geoff Stevens, 14

Chapter Three
WHILE YOU'RE WAITING...

Sometimes you can do more without being tied down!

Even though this book is largely about relating to guys, it's only logical that not everyone reading it will be *dating* someone, right? There's a good chance that you may not date much at all during your teen years. And you know what? That's perfectly OK!

Still... you see Amy and Bill together. And David and Amber are dating. Even Cheri and Alan are an item. You've heard it rumored that Brent and Allison are getting together—*and she just moved here!* Seems like everyone has someone... everyone, that is, except you. All your friends are pairing off with a guy, and the fact that you *don't* have a boyfriend has put you in a major slump.

Before you grab the Kleenex, let's have a girl-to-girl chat on this whole boyfriend thing, OK?

LEARNING TO TRUST

First of all, you have to come to the point of realizing that having a boyfriend isn't the most important thing in the world. What *is* most important is your relationship with Christ. Even though he designed you to *want* a boyfriend, he doesn't want your world to revolve around a relationship with a member of the opposite sex.

God knows your heart (he created it, remember?), and he takes great interest in everything that concerns you, including your romantic life. But he also wants you to give him *all* the desires you have.

When we place our wants, dreams, and desires into God's hands, we can relax and *know* that he is committed to meeting all our needs. Proverbs 3:5-6 says "Trust in the Lord with all your heart and lean not on your own understanding; in all your ways acknowledge him, and he will make your paths straight" (NIV).

When you feel left out because everyone has someone except you, remember that God is asking you to trust him to take care of all the details in your life—even in the boyfriend department. And your reward for placing him in complete control? He's promised to direct your paths. Remember, he has your best interests in mind. He won't lead you astray!

Keep in mind that it *could* be that God wants to do some special things in your life right now (while he has your complete attention) that he wouldn't be able to do if you were sidetracked with a boyfriend. This time of loneliness *can* be a wonderful time of exciting blessings... if you'll let it.

So don't use a whole box of Kleenex crying over what you

don't have. Instead, read on and see four reasons you can be *glad* you don't have a boyfriend right now. In fact, let's use the word *glad,* just to make it easier for me to explain and for you to remember.

G.L.A.D. TO BE SOLO

G. **Grow closer to God.** Many times when we're dating someone, it can be easy for us to slack off on our relationship with Christ. That is because it takes so much time and energy to develop a relationship, and that often leaves little room for our daily devotional time with him.

Basic truth: We're kidding ourselves if we think we can become strong in our faith without *daily* spending time praying and reading the Bible. The more time we spend with Christ, the stronger we become. But when we spend less of our time with him, our spiritual strength dissolves into weakness.

If you don't have a boyfriend, you're not distracted. Take advantage of this time to grow closer to Christ. Deepen your spiritual roots. Learn to strengthen your spiritual muscles. This is done by studying

Check out Colossians 2:7

the Bible, becoming more involved in church and youth group, and talking with others about Christ.

Check *this* out from Colossians 2:7: "Let your roots grow down into him and draw up nourishment from him. See that you go on growing in the Lord, and become strong and vigorous in the truth you were taught. Let your lives overflow with joy and thanksgiving for all he has done."

Grab a notebook—we'll call it your spiritual journal—and copy verses from the Bible that mean something special to you. Place a star by the Scriptures you'll try to memorize. Put a question mark by anything you don't understand and make a mental note to ask your parents or youth leader about it.

I'll list a few of *my* favorites to help get you started. Look up these verses and copy them in your spiritual journal:

☞ Ephesians 3:20
☞ 2 Corinthians 4:7-9
☞ Isaiah 41:10
☞ (Jot down a few of *your* favorites!)

Rejoice that God wants to do some exciting spiritual things in your life *right now!* If you had a boyfriend, you might not spend the time it takes to discover God's incredible spiritual surprises.

L **List your blessings.** When we're involved in a relation-ship, we can often be blinded to the wonderful things in our lives that God wants to help us focus on. This is a ter-rific time to list, count, and share our blessings.

Grab your spiritual journal and start by listing the blessings you receive from your family.

Family:

1. Dad works really hard to give the family what it needs.
2. Mom's a great cook.
3. My brother introduces me to his friends.
4. My sister lets me borrow her clothes every now and then.
5. Our family has some terrific holiday traditions.
6. (Keep going! List your own blessings!)

Now list the miscellaneous things you are grateful for. It could be anything, really. It could be things that come to mind instantly, or it could be things you really need to think about.

Other Stuff:

1. I love the feel of warm sunshine on my face.
2. I'm thankful for parades.
3. I'm glad I can worship God in a free country.
4. I'm grateful for cold lemonade on hot summer days.
5. I enjoy watching children giggle over things I view as ordinary.
6. (Keep going!)

A. **Authenticate your friendships.** A common mistake many girls make when they're involved in a relationship is ignoring their other friendships. They get so involved in the boyfriend that they don't make time to nurture and strengthen their *other* relationships.

Be glad you're not distracted with a boyfriend right now, because this gives you time to deepen your non-romantic friendships. To do that, let's put all of your friendships into three different categories. Try to decide who fits into which group, OK? If you need more space, grab that special notebook that you used to list your blessings.

Friends and acquaintances: These are people you know, but not especially well. You know their names, you say "hi" to them when you see them, but you don't actually fellowship together.

1. Lauren Leone   4. Heather Mac
2. John Lunn   5. Cristin Davis
3. Rob Flarety

Good friends: These are people you enjoy doing things with. You talk a lot with each other and you share things in common. You miss your good friends when they're not around.

1. _____Jane_____   4. _____Marilyn_____

2. _____Maura_____   5. _____Suzanne_____

3. _____Kendra_____

Intimate friends: These are the people with whom you share your secrets. You trust them. Intimate friends know you inside and out and are always there for you. You deeply care about these friends, and if they were hurting, you'd do anything you could to help them.

1. _____Shelley_____   4. _____Olivia_____

2. _____Bekah_____   5. _____Vi_____

3. _____Sarah_____

It takes a lot of time and effort to develop friendships with your acquaintances to the point that they become good friends. And it takes even more energy to develop your relationships with your good friends to where they become intimate friends. This is the level in which authentic and genuine relationships happen.

If you don't have a boyfriend right now, why not invest the time and effort it takes to improve your non-romantic friendships? Determine to authenticate your friendships by spending the time and energy necessary to move as many people as you can into that final category. These are the friends you'll cherish for a lifetime!

D: **Discover something about yourself.** If you don't have a relationship with a guy, you have a good supply of something that girls with boyfriends often don't have: time. Use this time to leap out and try new things. You don't have anyone holding you back, so go for it! Try to think of some things you've always wanted to try but haven't because you lacked the time.

Are you interested in crafts? Make a few things to sell at a local craft show or in a local craft shop. And what about reading? *Now* is a great time to dive into some books you never had time to read before. Wish you could read faster? Sign up for a speed-reading course. You'll be amazed at the results!

You could learn to play the guitar or take piano lessons. You could take the time to find out more about makeup and what your colors are. You could become a tennis player. The sky's the limit!

Be *glad* you're not tied down to a relationship, and do your best to explore your own personal interests. *Now* is the time to discover talents, abilities, and likes you never realized you had!

Remember, relationships take time and effort. Your friends who have boyfriends can't do all the things you can. So take advantage of the situation and use this time to become a more well-rounded person—someone the guy of your dreams can't help but like!

Do all guys believe that real men don't cry?

"No. Whoever said crying can't be a masculine trait? A lot of guys associate it with being a wuss, but people who say that aren't in touch with their feelings. A man who cries is a man who's confident—and secure enough in himself to express his emotions."

Donnie, 18

Why don't more Christian guys carry their Bibles to school?

"Most guys are concerned about how they look, and many think carrying a Bible doesn't look cool. They're afraid of being made fun of.

What's *really* gonna make a difference is not just toting a Bible around, but how you act. That says a lot more than what you carry."

Jason, 13

Why are guys always punching on each other?

"It's how we communicate with each other. You know how girls are always fixing each other's hair or tying or buttoning something for each other? They touch a lot—it's just their nature. Well, when we wrestle with each other or knock someone around, we're basically doing the same thing that girls are—only we're just more aggressive."

Matt, 17

Mail Bag 1
QUESTIONS AND ANSWERS ABOUT GUYS!

Dear Susie:

I'm fourteen and I'm going out with this guy who's not a Christian. He said he's interested, though. "Anything for you," were his words.

He's only been coming to my school since November, and ever since I met him I've had a feeling about him. I had been praying for God to send someone to love and encourage me, and since he does all that, I feel he's from God.

We have a great relationship and have set physical boundaries together. The problem? Well, we've kissed, and I feel guilty. My parents know and they say it's fine as long as I know and keep my boundaries and as long as the Lord is in our relationship. I feel weird, and I don't have good Christian friends.

Cypress, CA

I'm guessing you feel guilty because you've shared a very intimate part of yourself with someone who does not share your beliefs. And yes, even a *kiss* is an intimate expression of love.

37

Even though your boyfriend says "anything for you," that's not the right reason for becoming a Christian. If he claims to give his life to Christ because of you, it won't last very long.

We decide to commit our lives to God out of great love and gratitude for what he's done for us—not simply because our friends or dates have done it.

Your boyfriend needs his own personal, growing relationship with Jesus Christ—one that will continue long after you've both moved on to other dating partners.

Rethink whom you choose to go out with. My suggestion is to only date guys who share your faith, your values, and your pledge to remain sexually pure.

Dear Susie:

I'm the oldest of three girls. I'm twelve, and I've asked my mom several times if I can go out. And she's never really given me an answer. She's always saying that I'm getting cranky and having stomach aches, so I must be going through puberty. Doesn't that mean she thinks I'm old enough... but probably just doesn't want to tell me?

Mission Viejo, CA

You probably *are* going through puberty, but just because you're maturing physically doesn't necessarily mean that you're maturing emotionally. Ask your mom if the two of you can get alone on a Saturday afternoon and ask her specifically what signs of emotional maturity she feels are essential before you can begin dating.

As she begins to share specifics, you will have a chance to express your feelings of frustration. Explain that you want to begin establishing friendships with guys. Ask if you can invite some of your guy friends over to the house (while your family is present) or doing things in group situations—like bowling, videos, miniature golfing, etc.

Be sure you don't push your mom. If she feels you're trying to force her into allowing you to date, she may back off even further. Trust your parents to let you know when they feel the time is right.

Dear Susie:

There's this guy I really like—the problem is that he's one of my very best friends. He just thinks of me as a best friend. Sometimes he doesn't even see me as a girl. One time I put a little more makeup on than usual, and he said, "This is the first time I've seen you as a girl."

Is there anything I can do to get him to notice me as a girl he could go out with?

Clevelan, TX

Yes, there *are* a few things you can do. The next chapter offers some specifics, but let's start with this first: Maybe he needs to know that *you're* seeing *him* as more than a friend now, too.

You already know that the makeup caught his attention. Though you don't want to plaster it on, continue to do everything you can to make yourself look a little more special when you're around him. The more he sees your femininity, the faster he'll begin to realize that you could be much more than a friend.

Dear Susie:

I want to remain sexually pure until marriage. But what do you think about protected sex? If one or both of you are protected, I don't see how you'd be giving yourself to him.

                                                              Boston, MA

Protected sex is a lie! There is *no such thing* as protected sex outside of marriage. Oh, I know… you've heard all the advice about using a condom during sexual intercourse to protect you from AIDS. But did you know that the AIDS virus is actually 450 times smaller than sperm? When talking about condoms, doctors have compared it to water going through a fishnet! Do you really want to trust your life to a lousy piece of latex?

' "Giving yourself" to a guy is being sexually active. You say "I plan to remain sexually pure until marriage." What do you think sexual purity is? (See chapters thirteen and fourteen for more information on purity.)

If you're assuming simply because he'll be wearing a condom that you're not really having sex, you have a lot to learn. Sexual impurity involves a LOT more than intercourse.

Please talk to some Christian adults who can help you gain a correct view of what sexual involvement entails. I hope you'll save yourself… your *entire* self for your future husband.

Dear Susie:

I may be dating soon. But to be honest, I'm incredibly worried and scared about the whole thing. What's dating all about? I've never dated before, and I'm too embarrassed to ask my friends who have all dated plenty!

                                                              Tioga, ND

Dating is simply spending time with the opposite sex. Try to look at it as a friendship-building experience. Instead of barraging yourself with questions such as, "Does he like me?" "Will he ask me out again?" or "What's he thinking?" focus instead on simply becoming good friends.

Here's the big picture. Your guy friendships will determine the kinds of dating relationships you form. The dating relationships you have will likely influence your marriage relationship.

So it all starts with good solid guy friendships. Dates don't have to be expensive—though many are, and those are a lot of fun. But dates can be very informal as well. The issue is not how much money your evening costs. What's important is getting to know the person you're with... and *that* equals friendship.

Dear Susie:

Is it OK for a girl to ask one of her guy friends on a date? Not a serious or romantic date, but just to have fun and get to know one another? Or will he think that's being too pushy?

Ontario, CA

You say this guy is your friend, but you also say you want to ask him out to get to know him. If he's a good friend, you already know him well. It's my guess that he's really *not* a good friend yet, but you'd like him to be. Or he's a good friend, but you'd like him to be more than that.

I think whether he'd think you were being pushy is an individual thing. Some guys love it when a girl asks them to do something. Other guys are put off by it. That's why it's important to become good friends with him. By securing a great friendship, you'll know him so well you won't have to ask if he thinks you're being pushy.

Even more important that what *he* thinks, though, is what your *parents* think. They're the ones who have the final say in whether they want you to ask out guys. Talk to your mom about it and see if she has misgivings. It's my guess she'll probably point you in the right direction.

What annoys guys about girls?

"I once dated this girl who always agreed with me. She laughed at every joke and acted like everything I said was the coolest. I'd say 'What do you want to do tonight?' And she'd go, 'Whatever *you* want to do.' I like a girl who can think for herself."

Clay Crosse, contemporary Christian artist

What's the hardest thing that most guys your age are facing?

"Peer pressure. And that includes a TON of stuff... smoking, cheating, lying, sexual purity. I've made a commitment to steer clear of these things, but the pressure is still there."

Chad Stoltzfus, 16

What makes guys respect a girl?

"I have tremendous respect for a lady who has intelligently thought about her life—what she wants to do and how she'll accomplish it. This tells me she's secure. When a woman is sure of herself, I automatically respect her."

Eric Champion, contemporary Christian artist

Chapter Four
GETTING HIM TO NOTICE YOU

Catching a guy's attention doesn't have to be that difficult!

From the very moment you begin to notice guys, you begin to wonder just how to get him to notice you. It's a question nearly every woman has asked herself and her friends.

There are many ways to get guys to notice you, and all of them are things you can learn to do. It's just a matter of putting these things into practice.

The first thing we want to cover is your approachability. If you ever want guys to take interest in you, then you must be approachable. You know, someone a guy can feel comfortable approaching.

Some people are just naturally easier to talk to than others. But approachability is something *everyone* can learn. Most guys admit that they get a little nervous when trying to talk to girls. So, let's make it as easy as possible on them, OK?

APPROACHABILITY QUOTIENT

What kind of signals are *you* giving? Do you make it easy for a guy to talk to you? Or are you unconsciously making it uncomfortable for others to be around you? Let's test your approachability quotient! To find out just how approachable you are, take the following quick quiz.

1. You're getting books out of your locker and notice that Jody walks by three times. You...
   _✓_ a. turn and say, "Hi, Jody! How ya doin'?"
   ___ b. shut the door and walk on to class.

2. When eating lunch, you...
   ___ a. eat with a variety of people and try to leave at least one vacant seat at the table for someone else to use.
   _✓_ b. always eat with the same group of friends, and there are no empty seats around you.

3. When talking with friends before class, you...
   _✓_ a. look for other people you can include in the conversation.
   ___ b. keep to your own group of friends.

4. You're sitting in history class before the bell rings. Thad is sitting across from you with his head propped up by his hands. You ...
   _✓_ a. say, "Hey, Thad! Don't fall asleep! This is your most exciting, favorite class of the day... isn't it?"
   ___ b. slink down in your desk and wait for class to begin.

5. Jordan catches up with you in the hall as you're heading into science class. "You going to the game tomorrow?" he asks. You...

   ✓ a. say, "I want to. Are you going?"

   __ b. say, "I don't know," and walk on.

6. You see some guy friends hanging out in the hall before school. You...

   ✓ a. walk over and say, "Hi! You guys get your home-work done?"

   __ b. walk past them and try to find your locker partner.

7. Benji never goes to the library unless he's forced to. This is one of those times. Your entire English class has to do research. You notice Benji is having a hard time figuring out how to find the right information. He looks your way and catches your eye. You...

   ✓ a. smile and say, "Libraries can be kinda confusing sometimes. Can I help you find something?"

   __ b. look quickly away and continue searching for your own information.

SCORING

If you answered mostly A's, you're approachable. Guys will feel comfortable talking to you, and they should enjoy seek-ing out your company.

But if you answered mostly B's, then guys won't always be sure if you want them to talk to you or not. You sometimes appear to be preoccupied or too busy to stop and show inter-est in others.

Repeat after me: *Guys are usually nervous when approaching a girl, so the easier I can make it for him, the* *more comfortable he'll feel talking with me.*

Now that we're clear on being more approachable, let's get to the "meat" of the issue... How do I get him to notice me?

GETTING HIS ATTENTION

You've known Jeff since third grade, but all of a sudden he looks... *different!* You've just begun another school year, and Jeff has just entered your homeroom. You can't believe your eyes. Wow! you think. Has this guy been working out, or what?

The gangly Jeff you said good-bye to last spring has sprung into a hunk! Whatever he did over the summer (mow lawns, haul supplies, construction work) sure made a difference in how he looks, because he's certainly not gangly anymore. Jeff has filled out, grown taller, and he has an incredible tan.

Your heart beats a little faster, and for the first time you really notice Jeff... you and every other girl in your class. And who can help but notice him? He carries himself with confidence, he's got killer eyes and a smile to die for.

You find yourself daydreaming about him during biology. You look for him between classes, and you memorize where he sits in the cafeteria. Why the sudden attraction? Why can't you get him off your mind? What's going on inside of you?

You're being normal, that's what. See, God created you to feel attracted to members of the opposite sex. It's OK to notice that Jeff has filled out. Why wouldn't you be attracted to him? He's a good-looking guy with a great personality. So, take a deep breath and realize that what you're feeling is part of what makes you a woman.

Now that we've settled *that,* the major question you want to zero in on is, "How do I get Jeff to notice me?" Here are a few quick suggestions on how to spark the interest:

1. Be more than a buddy. If you've known this guy for a while, chances are he may think of you as just one of his buddies. But you don't want to be "one of the guys." In order for him to see you as anything more than a pal, he needs to be reminded of your femininity—something his male friends don't have!

Instead of plunging through the door in front of him, pause and wait for him to open it for you. Now, I realize all women who scream "equal rights!" would say this goes against everything they believe in. I believe in equal rights related to work: If a female is doing the same job a male is, and her job performance is equal, she should be paid the same amount.

But in other situations, I believe our roles need to be taken from the Bible. And God has clearly designed the man to be the stronger of the two sexes. There are times when a woman should depend on a man, and letting a guy open doors for you is simply enjoying a courteous gesture.

Remember, you want him to make a clear distinction between you and his male buddies. (I'm mentioning this "door thing" more than once in this book, because I don't want you to skim quickly over it then forget it. I think it's important.)

When you're trying to get a guy to stop seeing you as a pal, you need to make him put out effort to see you. Here's what I mean:

A guy probably doesn't have to give his male friends much advance notice when he wants to do something with them. And if you've been friends with him for a while, you've probably done a few things together, too. But now that you're wanting him to see you as more than a friend, don't make it so easy on him. In other words, if it's always convenient to be with you, he'll never have to work at it.

Guys enjoy a challenge, so don't be available every time he calls. Always be friendly, and always let him know you're interested, but tell him that sometimes you need more than thirty minutes notice. He'll quickly get the message that you're not one of the guys.

2. Dress for success. If you have been buddies for a while, you'll probably be very comfortable hanging out in your sweats with him. But if you want him to see you as more than a pal, you can reflect that wish in how you dress.

Wearing a dress or a cute skirt sets you apart from someone in grubbies.

Many girls make the mistake of trying to catch a guy's attention by dressing provocatively. Guys who see girls wearing clothes that fit too tight or are cut too low stereotype them into one category: easy. You want a guy to like you for who you are, not for what you can show him. Anyone can dress suggestively, but a guy respects a girl who dresses well, looks good in what she wears, and can turn his head with her knock-out personality.

In addition to dressing nicely, you can also try something different with your hair, experiment with new makeup, or borrow a favorite blouse from a friend. Half the fun of catching a guy's attention is the challenge. Enjoy it!

3. Watch your body language. Take a quick inventory of your body language. When you're around him, what's your body doing? How are you sitting? Are you acting like a lady? Do you plop down into a chair like one of the guys? Do you appear to be interested in his conversation? Again, here is where your femininity has a chance to show itself.

When I taught high school, a girl in one of my classes was named Ann. She was friends with everyone, and all the guys thought of her as their buddy. She was always ready for a pick-up game of basketball, and she was good!

I watched her during class. She joked with all the guys, and she acted just like them! When they wanted someone to run around with, they chose Ann. But when they wanted a date, they asked Jenny, Debbi, or a number of other girls.

Why was it that nobody wanted to ask Ann for a date? It was because Ann was too much like them. They wanted to take a young lady to the banquet or the concert—someone who acted a little more feminine.

Jenny, Debbi, and many other girls who were asked to the special events were also athletic. They ran track and played softball, but they never lost their femininity. When they sat down, they sat like ladies. They were careful and watchful of what their bodies were saying.

4. "Extra" doesn't have to be extravagant. Try to think of ways you can get his attention that are different from his male friends. For example, if he's on the track team, take a bottle of cold Gatorade to the practice field and leave a short note with it: "Have a great practice!" Clearly his guy buddies aren't going to be bringing him cold drinks!

If he has a part-time job, take a batch of freshly baked cookies (or carrot and celery sticks if he's a health nut) for him to snack on during break time. Small gestures of kindness will catch his attention without making him think you're after him.

5. Learn the art of conversation. The best way to capture and keep a guy's attention is simply to talk to him.

If you're not sure of your conversational skills, then it might help for you to come up with a mental list of things ahead of time that you'd like to talk to him about. Start with some simple questions, such as: "How'd you do on the math quiz?" "Are you going to the football game this Friday?" "You'll never guess what our youth group is planning!"

After you've worked from a list a few times, you'll learn to become more comfortable thinking on your feet. You'll be able to make conversation with him spontaneously.

One more quick piece of advice for you when you start making conversation with a guy: Even though you might feel nervous talking with him, try to appear confident. Everyone enjoys conversing with someone who feels good about herself. Don't hog the conversation, but just see where it goes naturally. (Read more about this in chapter five.)

6. Smile a lot. Have you ever noticed how guys are attracted to girls who smile? That's because guys (and gals, too) are drawn to positive people. Think about the people you enjoy being around the most. They're probably people who enjoy smiling and laughing, right? We all love hanging out with friends who have a good attitude and enjoy laughing.

The more you smile, the better you'll feel. Honest! Try it. (Right now. Go ahead.) Feels good, doesn't it? A smile always puts others at ease. People who smile are usually noticed above everyone else. So dare to stand out—smile!

7. Always be friendly. Probably the most important thing in catching a guy's attention is simply to be nice. Make a point to say "hi" when you pass him in the hallway. If you know what kinds of activities he's involved in, ask him about them. This shows that you're interested in what he's doing.

There's nothing more refreshing to a guy who's having a bad day than being cheered up by a friendly face. Everyone needs more friends.

A FINAL WORD

The subject of friendliness brings us back to where we started. If you've been friends with him in the past but now want something more, keep on keepin' on. In other words, don't quit being his friend if he *doesn't* come around. Even if he starts dating someone else, determine to continue being friendly. After all, it might be the next school year that he notices you in a new light for the very first time!

Why do guys just toss stuff into their lockers instead of stacking it neatly?

"Because we're usually in a hurry, and it takes too much time to stack it. Who's gonna look in your locker, anyway? It's not like this is my 'home away from home' or something.

"Girls care more about how their lockers look than guys do. I hang up a few pics of friends or sports celebs, but that's it."

Joey, 14

What do you do to spice up your devotional life?

"I choose a topic I want to know more about, read up on it, research the Word, then record my thoughts and ideas on what I believe.

"I just finished reading *The Republic* by Plato. I looked up Scripture references and gained a lot of insight about different views of reality. Then I took my notes and did a comparison study on heaven."

Steve, 18

Chapter Five

TALKING TO GUYS

Communicating with the opposite sex doesn't have to be a nightmare!

> I want to talk to him, but I don't have anything to say!

Many girls I know feel nervous and uncomfortable about talking to guys. The following letter is typical of many I receive.

Dear Susie:

I have a big problem—boys scare me half to death! Whenever I'm around my boyfriend, I clam up, even though I have a million things to say. My heart hammers, and I feel really stupid. Why do I feel this way, and how can I overcome it?

Grand Rapids, Mich.

The first thing I would tell the writer of this letter is to just relax and realize that her feelings are completely normal. Probably every girl in the world has felt this way.

GUY TALK

How We Want Girls To Talk To Us

"It would probably be uncomfortable to be approached by a girl who just walks up and says 'hi' but doesn't have anything else to talk about. Try to think ahead of time about what you'll say. Have something specific in mind (homework, church, last Friday's football game)."

—Ryan, 17

"If we're wearing something cool, it can serve as a good ice-breaker, because you can comment on that particular item. Or if we *have* something you like, talk about that. For instance, a car or a surfboard would be good things to ask about."

—Benjamin, 16

"If you've just met the guy, ask simple questions like 'What school do you go to?' 'Where do you live?' 'What church do you attend?' Above all, relax. Don't be scared; we won't bite."

—Chuck, 17

"If you have a class at school together, use *that* to start a conversation. Ask questions about the class and homework assignments or how he did on a specific test.

"You could also ask about his hobbies and interests, but don't just say, 'So... what are your hobbies and interests?' You don't want it to sound like a survey or something."

—Peter, 13

"All a girl has to ask is 'How are you doing?' As the conversation continues, we'll probably clue in that you like us. Please don't be afraid to talk to us. Who knows? Maybe we like you, too, and are just too afraid to show it."

—Keith, 14

"I *love* to talk about sports. So if a girl starts a conversation with sports in it, I'm hooked!"

—Mike, 15

"I like it when a girl calls just to chat. Maybe she'll wish me happy birthday or just wants to see what I'm doing. This gets a casual conversation started and makes it easy for me to talk with her."

—Jerry, 16

"Questions that force us to give our opinions are good. Try not to ask simple yes/no questions if you want a good conversation. Ask questions about things we might have in common, like church, school, or friends."

—Paul, 15

"Don't talk too much about yourself. Guys hate that! Try to find some common ground and talk about things you both enjoy."

—Alan, 14

"I was at a party, and nothing was planned, so this girl and I started having a conversation about our beliefs. We talked about abortion, the afterlife, women's rights, liberals, and a whole lot more.

"We had a great time and got to know each other a lot better. So if you're really wanting to get to know a guy on a deeper level, ask questions about stuff that really matters."

—Kris, 16

But talking to boys is just like anything else that makes you nervous when you first try it. Believe me, if you don't give up, it *will* get easier. The more you're around boys, the more comfortable you'll become.

There are many ways to overcome your fear. For instance, instead of putting yourself in situations where you're alone with your boyfriend, try staying in group situations. That way you can coast on the conversation of others and won't feel as much pressure to do as much talking.

The following fiction story was written to offer girls insight about communicating with the opposite sex. I've included it here because it provides some hints that you may find helpful.

A LITTLE BOOK LEARNIN'

Susan sat in her English class, listening to Mrs. Crackett discuss the finer points of creative writing. Although Susan liked this part of English best, she still found it difficult to keep her mind on the subject at hand that day. The hands on the clock showed only three minutes before fourth period, but lunch wasn't the only thing on her mind.

Jason seemed to catch everything Mrs. Crackett had to say. From where Susan was sitting, she had just the right view of the slight wave in his brown hair. Why was it that just the thought of trying to talk to a guy like Jason always made her nervous? It wasn't that she wanted to ask him out on a date. She just wanted to talk to him. But the thought of starting a conversation with him terrified her.

She remembered the time Brian wanted to go steady with her in the sixth grade. He had talked to her best friend Karen, and she had passed the request on to Susan. She didn't even know Brian—or *like* him for that matter. But she'd never gone with a guy before, so she told Karen to tell him "OK."

It had been completely painless. He never bothered to call

her on the phone or even sit next to her. They didn't have a single conversation during the week of their "relationship," but at least she could say she had gone steady once in her life.

But that all seemed pretty silly now. She might as well send away for a boyfriend through the mail. All she really wanted was to learn how to talk to a boy without feeling like she was going to lose her lunch.

Riiiiiingg!

As class ended, Susan watched Jason pick up his books and move toward the quad. She thought about how nice it would be to sit and talk with him in the cafeteria. She had no trouble talking to girls, so why the big problem with boys? It really didn't make sense to her.

"Susan! Ready for lunch?" Karen interrupted her thoughts.

"Sure," Susan said as they walked into the hallway together. "You know, I was just thinking that somebody ought to write a book on how girls can learn to talk to guys."

Karen got a funny look on her face, so funny that Susan had to ask what was going on. "What's wrong?" she asked.

"Nothing. I just happen to have in my possession *the very book* you want. Got it last night at Bower's Books." She held up a thin copy of *Miss Marvelous' Secrets for Talking to Guys*. Susan couldn't believe it. There was an actual book on the subject of talking to guys!

Susan took the booklet from her friend and leafed through it, glancing at its suggestions.

"Can I borrow this?"

That night Susan read the book, devouring these suggestions for talking to boys:

1. **"Start by looking good,"** she read. "If you don't feel good about how you look, you'll probably feel embarrassed when you try to talk to a guy. It's important to look your very best."

Susan had never thought about that, but she

knew Miss Marvelous was probably right. If she felt good about herself, it was more likely that any boy she talked to would also feel good toward her.

2. "Don't tell yourself you're shy. You have a tendency to become what you think you are. So tell yourself you are an outgoing person who likes to talk to other people. By *acting* confident you'll soon begin to believe in your ability to talk to others."

Susan felt like that part had been written just for her. She always saw herself as a shy person who would rather sit and let the world go by, rather than get involved. And since she *saw* herself as a shy person, she *acted* like a shy person. She could see the importance of seeing herself as an outgoing person.

Miss
Marvelous
says:

3. "Prepare what you're going to say ahead of time. Fear often comes from not knowing what you're going to say beforehand. If you can plan out your words in certain situations—before they come up—you won't find yourself at a loss for something to say."

That made sense. Susan often found herself without anything to say. She always hated it when someone would say to her, "What's wrong? Why aren't you saying anything?" But if she planned the situations she might find herself in, and figured out what to say ahead of time, she wouldn't end up just standing there, looking like a jerk.

4. "Learn how to make small talk. Life is full of ordinary things, but sometimes we think we can't talk about them. Most conversations are composed of a lot of talk about little things. To keep a conversation going, it's important to know how to talk about average stuff."

Susan thought about all those times when her attempts at conversation with guys seemed dull and boring. The problem, she now realized, was that she didn't have anything to say about the little things of life. She decided she would try to become better at small talk. She thought it might be good for her to practice with Karen.

5. "Be interested in what a guy is interested in. Everyone likes to talk to people who show an interest in their opinions and experiences. Boys are no different. Being interested in what they have to say is a good beginning to most conversations. Learn to be interested in sports and subjects that hold high interest for guys."

Susan smiled. She liked baseball and kept up with the National League standings. Her father had taken her to a Cubs game last year, and she was anxious to follow *her team* this year—maybe all the way to the World Series. Perhaps she could use her interest in baseball as a source of conversation starters.

The next day at school, Susan expressed a brand-new confidence. She felt she could talk to *anyone*. As she approached her locker, she noticed Roger getting a drink from the water fountain. Although they had never talked before, they had science class together.

"Hi, Roger," she said brightly.

"Oh, hi." He looked surprised.

"What are you doing for a science project?" she asked, beginning to work her locker combination.

"I'm doing a study on weather forecasting. Why?"

"Oh, you do so well in science I just wanted to know what your project was." Roger's face almost glowed as he explained the details.

Susan smiled. She was actually enjoying the conversation *without the slightest feeling of a nervous stomach.*[1]

1. John Souter, "How to Talk to Guys," *Brio*, March 1990.

SO IT ALL COMES DOWN TO...

The bottom line is: Guys *want* to be your friend. And they like it when you show interest in them just as much as you do when they show interest in you.

And it's really not as difficult to start conversations with guys as you might make yourself believe. Try using some of the same conversational skills you would in striving to make friends with a girl. Of course, you probably won't get too far talking about the sale on pajamas at J.C. Penney's. But the general principles for carrying on good conversation are pretty much the same to both sexes.

Start out learning to be comfortable talking to both boys and girls. The more comfortable you become talking to people in general, the more at ease you'll feel when striking up a new conversation with a guy.

Why do so many guys wear a cross?

"I guess it's sort of the *in* thing right now. And it's not just guys—it's girls, too. But *wearing* something doesn't mean *anything*. Even Prince wears a cross! And get this—Madonna prays before concerts. Gimme a break! Her prayer is, 'Oh, God, make me as sexy as I can be.' So it's not necessarily what you *say* or *do*; it's whether or not you're living a life for Christ that makes the difference."

Kirk Sullivan, 4HIM

Chapter Six

FIVE WAYS TO BE A *Great* FRIEND TO A GUY

It doesn't take as much as you might think to secure a good friendship with a guy!

One of the most exciting things in life is establishing quality friendships with the opposite sex. Though it's important to have lots of same-sex friends, many times you'll find that friendships with the *opposite* sex can help you develop some essential social skills that you'll need for healthy dating relationships.

Check out Matthew 12:34-35

The problem for many of us, though, is that we really don't know how to establish these friendships. If *you're* wondering how to develop a solid girl/guy friendship, here are five fantastic ways to make any guy want to be your friend:

1. Spread positive gossip. Everyone has *something* positive that you can focus on and talk about. Strive to look for and talk about the good things in all people, including your guy friends. Think about the things you admire most about your guy friend, and spread them around! Learn to be a positive gossiper.

Aaron answered a tough question in math class today? Why not tell somebody? Mitch did great at football practice after school? Spread it around. You saw Joel talking to a new kid? Tell others that he's good at reaching out. The more positive gossip you can spread, the more people will be attracted to you.

Everyone likes to be around someone who's full of good news. When a guy finds out you're a positive gossiper and that you enjoy saying nice things about him, he'll feel he can trust you, because he knows you'll choose to talk about the good things in others and not the bad. What a great reputation to have!

To remind yourself to spread good news, hang this verse inside your locker: "For a man's heart determines his speech. A good man's speech reveals the rich treasures within him" (Matthew 12:34-35).

2. Include him in your conversations. You've been there: You're standing around with a group of about five friends and only three of them are really involved in the conversation, and you're not one of those three. It's not that you don't want to be a part of it all... it's just that they're not including you. Frustrating, huh? Especially when you're all standing there together!

If you want to be a good friend with a guy, include him in your conversations. Many girls *don't* do this because they feel uncomfortable and don't know *how* to involve the guy standing around in what they're saying.

But a guy will seek to be around the girl who works at including *everyone* in what's going on. No one wants to feel like they're on the outside looking in. The more you can include your guy friends, the more they'll want to hang around you.

3. Seek his advice. Mindy was having problems at home. It seemed her parents always let her older brother have more freedom than they allowed her to have. She felt as though her parents just didn't trust her, and that hurt and frustrated her.

Bryce wondered if something was bothering Mindy, and during lunch he asked her if she needed to talk about anything. She began to share what she was going through.

"It seems so unfair," she said. "My parents are really terrific, but I just don't think they realize how I feel."

"It could be that they're just being protective of you," Bryce said, "which has nothing at all to do with trust."

"What do you mean?" Mindy asked.

"Well," he said, "it seems that so many rotten things happen to girls today. I mean, they can hardly walk home after school alone. We're always hearing about a girl being attacked, raped, kidnapped, or killed. It's not fair, but girls are just more vulnerable. They can't always fight against a man who's sick-o and determined to do something malicious."

"That's true," Mindy agreed. She hadn't thought of this perspective before.

"So I don't think it's that your parents don't trust you," Bryce said. "The truth is, they're probably crazy in love with you and just don't want you to get hurt. But your older brother... well, he's more capable of defending himself. Or at least, it's not as likely he'd be attacked if he walked home alone after school."

"Yeah, I understand that. But it still doesn't change how I feel."

"Why don't you sit down with your folks *and* your brother and see if there's some kind of compromise you can all agree upon?"

"Yeah," Mindy said. "That's a good idea. I think I will. Thanks, Bryce. You're a good listener, and you give pretty good advice."

"Hey, that's what good friends are for," he said. "Come on. Let's get to English class."

Everyone likes to be needed. When you seek the advice of your guy friend, you're letting him know you trust him enough to help you with something important. Don't misuse this, and don't unload on him every time you're together. But go ahead and talk things over with him when you need to. He may be able to help you see your problem in a new perspective by giving you his male viewpoint.

4. Have a listening ear.
You know how *you* need someone to talk to sometimes? Well, it's the same with your guy friend. Let your guy friend know that it's safe for him to talk to you about what *he's* dealing with in his life. Give him the freedom to talk to you without having to worry about your motivation. If he thinks you're going to start flirting with him when he tells you that he's having second thoughts about asking Linda out, he probably won't share *anything* with you again. He needs to know that his secrets are safe with you.

When he confides in you, don't take advantage of what you know by trying to turn it to your good. If he's having problems with another friend who is also a girl, don't jump in with, "Yeah, Jeannie's a two-faced snob. You deserve better." He doesn't need that. He *does* need a listening ear.

Hear him out. Offer your heart-felt suggestions and the best advice you can give. If you create this kind of comfortable friendship with him, he'll know it's safe to spill his guts. There's not a guy in the world who wouldn't cherish a friend like that. And when *you're* having problems with a guy friend, who do you think is going to be right by your side making sure you're not hurt or in too deep over your head? That's right... this guy friend who feels comfortable with you because you listen.

5. Sprinkle on the smiles.
Though it's OK to share your frustrating moments with close friends, you want to be careful that

you're not *always* unloading on your guy friend. No one likes to be around someone who's down all the time.

Guys enjoy girls who are fun, who smile a lot. Be willing to laugh at yourself. If you trip on something when you walk into class or drop your lunch tray in the cafeteria, instead of feeling like crawling in a hole and wanting to die, tell your guy friend about it and laugh it away. He'll admire your sense of humor and the fact that you're secure enough not to worry about it.

IN CONCLUSION...

Again, establishing good, solid friendships with the opposite sex is one of the most special things in life. *Every* friendship takes work—even your friendships with other girls. Be willing to invest time and effort in developing deep friendships. *Treasure* your guy friends and don't take them for granted.

GUY TALK

I Love It When Girls...

"I love it when a girl enjoys coming over to my house and talking with my parents. I also enjoy being around girls who are honest about their walk with Christ. I want them to talk about God and offer a mature Christian perspective to problems encountered.

"A lot of girls are timid about eating in front of guys. They worry about what the guy is thinking while they're eating. I love it when a girl feels good enough about herself to really enjoy the meal I've treated her to."

—Kent, 17

"I love to be around girls who have a good sense of humor. I'm not talking about the ones who just giggle at everything... there's a BIG difference. A giggler tends to be dingy. A girl with a good sense of humor can usually hold up her own end of the conversation.

"I think it's important that she be able to laugh at herself, too. This tells me she's confident and has a good self-image. Girls who are always worried about how they look usually have a low self-esteem and aren't much fun to be around."

—Tim, 16

"I love it when a girl doesn't always agree with me. I want to know what she thinks. As we exchange ideas and opinions it challenges each of us.

"I want God to be the center of my dating relationships. Therefore, I love to pray together or discuss something from the Bible. I'm *not* suggesting a one-on-one Bible study with your date, because I think there's a danger in this. It's too easy to get distracted. It's also easy to confuse this deeper level of intensity with your feelings for the person next to you.

"I love it, though, when a girl shares what God is teaching her. This challenges me to look harder at my own life."

—Dave, 17

"I love it when girls really dress nice for a date. It makes the guy feel special and appreciated. Girls who dress revealing, though, must feel they have to do something extra to get guys to notice them. I wish they realized they're advertising a low self-concept. It's hard for guys to keep a clean mind and pure thoughts when girls dress that way.

"I love it when a girl shows off her *high* morals by dressing appropriately and looking nice."

—Shane, 18

Why are guys so competitive?

"It's just part of our nature. I *hate* losing. It's a guy thing... sort of our instinct. Probably goes back to caveman days when guys had to compete for food, shelter, women—everything... even life! Part of this attitude just carries over today."

Chad Kendall, 18

Why is it important for guys to be involved in church?

"It's important for *me* because I want to hang out with other Christians. I need spiritual support from other kids my age. Getting involved in church also helps me establish the right kind of values. Plus, just being with other Christians our age helps us learn how to relate to each other better. Church isn't just for spiritual growth; it's great for *social* growth.."

Todd Johnson, 14

Chapter Seven
WHAT DO GUYS WANT IN A RELATIONSHIP

Tired of the guessing games? Here's the scoop!

Do you ever feel confused about what guys *really* want?

Yo! It's like this...

Maria, your older sister, says guys want someone who is feminine and dainty. Your cousin, Leslie, says they want someone dumber than they are so they won't feel threatened. And Kimberly? She says guys just want someone they can kiss. And she's dated about every guy in the school, so maybe she knows what she's talking about....

Instead of taking in what everyone else is saying, let's take a quick quiz and find out how much *you* know. Just how well *do* you read guys? This is a true-false quiz, so you know the routine!

1. When Jerry asked Sarah to ride bikes with him on Saturday, she made sure she used enough hair spray to keep her hair looking great for him all afternoon. After all, that's what guys want, right?

2. Guys like to do most of the talking when they're with a girl.

3. Lisa aced her science test, but when Ronnie asked how she did, she hid her paper. *If he finds out I made an A when he's struggling so much, he'll quit talking to me,* she thought. Lisa believed that guys don't like girls who make better grades than they do.

4. If something's bothering a guy, it's smart to ask him about it.

5. Juli won first place in the art talent contest over the weekend. When Paul asked her on Monday how she did, she said, "OK, I guess. Those things are underrated." *If he finds out how good I am, he'll lose interest in me,* she thought. Guys really don't like girls who are good at the things they do.

6. Guys like it when you do something special for them.

7. Mark is running for class president. Erica has painted posters for him, given suggestions on a campaign speech and showed up at his house twice last week to offer more help. Today is election day. *He'll love it,* she thought, *if I deliver a singing telegram wishing him luck during first period.* Guys like big, splashy things like that.

8. Phil and Terri had made plans to play tennis. As soon as his car pulled into the driveway, she ran out to meet him. *Guys don't like having to get out and come up to the door to get a girl,* she thought. Guys really don't like having to go to that kind of trouble.

9. Damon was complaining to Rachel about how unfair Mr. Green was being with his math grade. Rachel readily agreed with him. Later, when Damon mentioned how lame the band that had played for the school assembly was, Rachel

agreed again. *After all,* she thought, *guys want someone who will agree with them, not give them flak.* Guys don't like girls who have minds of their own.

10. Guys are attracted to girls who wear lots of makeup.

Answers

1. *False.* Guys like to have fun, so therefore they enjoy being with a girl who likes to have fun too. If Jerry had asked Sarah to dinner or to a concert, she would have wanted to make sure her hair looked great the entire evening. But riding bikes? Your hair's *supposed* to blow! Chances are Jerry won't ask her to do something that fun again. He'll sense that she's too worried about how she looks to have a good time.

2. *False.* Even though they may not show it, most guys are pretty nervous around girls. Though they don't want a girl to hog the conversation, any guy will admit he's relieved when a girl can hold her own when talking with him. That's why it's so important to learn good conversational skills. Guys love to talk, but they need a little nudging every now and then, and they enjoy well-rounded conversations that aren't one-sided.

3. *False.* If a guy *is* intimidated by the fact that you make better grades than he does, he's not worth going after. Repeat after me: "I will NEVER play dumb just to get a guy's attention." If you do, you're in worse shape than the guy is.

4. *True.* If you notice Bryan just doesn't seem like himself today, ask him if everything's OK. If he says he's fine, but you still suspect something's bothering him, jot him a quick note to let him know you care, then DROP THE SUBJECT. Asking once or twice is enough. No one likes to be nagged. But guys love it when girls show concern about what's going on in their lives. This tells him you're sensitive, observant, and caring.

5. *False.* Guys enjoy being with a girl they can be proud of. Juli would have been proud of Paul for placing at the state track meet. Likewise, he'd love to share her happiness in taking first place at the art competition. Guys want to rejoice with you. Laughing together and sharing the good times serve to bring two people closer together. Don't brag about yourself or flaunt things, but don't be afraid about sharing your accomplishments, either.

6. *True. Anyone* enjoys a little special attention—it makes us feel important. You don't have to do anything expensive or extravagant, but a little something every now and then to let your guy friend know you appreciate his friendship will make him feel significant.

7. *False.* Obviously, Erica doesn't know when too much is too much. Though guys like to feel important, no one enjoys being doted over. If Mark really appreciated her help, he would have thanked her for what she's already done. There's such a thing as too *much* attention. By constantly being available, Erica has taken all the challenge away from Mark. There's nothing left for him to pursue.

Giving a fun reminder of appreciation *every once in a while* (as mentioned in the previous question) is different than throwing yourself at a guy. As soon as elections are over, Mark won't need Erica any longer and will start avoiding her.

8. *False.* Guys enjoy treating a girl like a lady. Opening doors for her, picking her up from her porch instead of the curb or driveway, and meeting her parents are all a part of the dating game. Any guy you're thinking of dating needs to meet your parents. If he doesn't want to meet them, he isn't worth dating!

9. *False.* Guys enjoy a girl who uses her own mind. If you always agree with everything the guy says and does, it's no fun

for him. Most guys enjoy smart conversations, so they like a girl with her own opinions and the ability to make decisions on her own. This provides a fun and stimulating challenge for the guy. And if he feels challenged, he'll come back for more. If you nod your head "yes" to all that he says, he'll get bored and look around for a more stimulating friendship.

10. *False.* Guys like girls who look good. Plastering your face with tons of makeup looks phony. Most guys are attracted to a girl who knows how to use makeup to enhance her *natural* beauty.

ALL IN ALL....

We've discussed several situations and how most guys respond to them. But more than remembering the answers to this quiz, you know what's *really* important? BEING YOURSELF!

All guys enjoy being around girls who are comfortable with themselves. See, when you can relax and simply be *you,* then you don't have to cake your face with extra makeup or ramble on and on about stuff you don't even care about or worry about your grades or wonder if you're popular enough or cute enough or athletic enough or write run-on sentences to keep a guy's attention! All you have to do is simply be YOU. When that happens, chances are you'll have lots of guys wanting to be your friend.

So keep reading... and we'll talk about how to be such a good friend to a guy that he'll value your friendship for a long time!

Mail Bag II
QUESTIONS AND ANSWERS ABOUT GUYS!

Dear Susie:

What do guys like to talk about when they're out with a girl?

Ontario, Canada

Though they don't like to talk about *everything* girls do (shopping, fingernail polish, hair styles), they DO enjoy talking about many of the same things: favorite TV shows and movies, current events, God, school, hobbies.[1]

Dear Susie:

I know that sex before marriage is totally wrong, so I wouldn't even consider it. But, is kissing wrong? I like kissing my boyfriend. I'm thirteen years old. I don't want to do anything that's displeasing to God because I'm a Christian. Am I sinning when I kiss him?

Moore, OK

1.For specific things to talk about, grab a copy of *Opening Lines* by Susie Shellenberger and Greg Johnson; Broadman & Holman publishers.

I don't believe kissing is a sin, but I would like to encourage you to be careful in giving away *any* physical affection. You see, anytime we're physically involved (even slightly) with the opposite sex, it works like a glue that bonds us closer together. Even holding hands with your boyfriend will make you feel more connected to him.

No, I don't believe you're sinning when you kiss your boyfriend, but let me ask you to guard yourself. For instance, if you kiss for prolonged periods of time, kissing can lead to petting. And petting can lead to intercourse—and that's how girls who never intended to give away their virginity lose it before marriage.

I'm not saying you're headed for sex. I *am* asking you to be smart. Don't spend a lot of time alone together. Don't allow yourself to become comfortable with prolonged and deep kissing. Sooner or later, that won't be enough, and you'll want to go a step further.

God created the desires within you that you're experiencing. You enjoy kissing your boyfriend because it feels good, and that's normal. Just realize that it will also connect you in a powerful way. Don't do so much that you'll live with regret when a breakup comes. We should all be able to look at our past relationships and have nothing to be ashamed of.

Dear Susie:

There's this guy at my church that I have a HUGE crush on. I've been in love with him my whole life, but I've never told him.

Several people at church have said they think he likes me too, but I'm not sure. I really want to talk to him and tell him how I feel, but I'm kind of shy and so is he.

Everyone thinks we'd make a good couple. Please give me some advice on how to talk to him about it.

Canonsburg, PA

I'm glad you've chosen to set your sights on a guy at church. I realize not everyone who goes to church is a Christian, but the chances are higher when you date someone from church, he'll come closer to sharing your beliefs and your values.

Other people have told you they think you'd make a great couple. It feels good to hear people say that, doesn't it? It affirms our womanhood. It makes us feel feminine and attractive.

But the bottom line is not really what *they* think but what *he* thinks. You probably won't like my answer, since you want advice on how to talk with him. But here goes: It isn't your place to let him know how you feel. Again, the issue is how HE feels. If he's attracted to you and is interested in getting to know you as more than a friend, he'll eventually do something about it. If he's shy, it may take him a while. But let *him* do the approaching.

I know that's hard to hear. It's tough to wait around on a guy, isn't it? But deep down, wouldn't you much rather the initial move come from him? That way you *know* he likes you. If *you* make the first move, you'll always question whether he just went along with it, or if he really, really, really likes you.

Dear Susie:

I have a boyfriend who's a year younger than me. All my friends hate him because they think he's ugly. I'm losing all my friends because of him. Shouldn't they be looking at what's inside of him? Should I dump him and get my friends back, or should I just lose all my friends?

Alberta, Canada

I admire you for looking past the outside package and into this guy's character. You know what's funny? The guys who aren't that great-looking in junior high or high school come back to their school reunions ten years later, looking knock-dead gorgeous! Their bodies have filled out, they've learned how to style their hair, and they're usually the ones who have started their own businesses or become successful... and every unattached female there is making a fool out of herself to be introduced to them.

If your friends are dumping you because you're not dating a hunk, they're not actually friends at all. REAL friends rejoice in the pleasures of others. In other words, if your friends were *real*, instead of dissing him, they'd be happy *with* you for dating a neat guy full of character. Look for some new friends.

Dear Susie:

I've liked this guy for quite some time now, but I'm not sure if he likes me. Is it better not to do anything and let the guy initiate it?

It seems whenever I like someone, God points me in the other direction, saying this isn't the right guy. Will the right guy ever come along?

Ontario, Canada

I admire your tender heart toward God's leading. I also assume you want his very best for your life. Instead of seeing this "direction changing" as a frustration, try to view it as his loving way of keeping you headed in the right direction.

For instance, if you knew where a stash of gold was hidden, and you wanted your parents to have it, yet were forbidden to tell anyone where it was verbally, you'd try your best to guide them in the right direction.

If the stash was hidden underneath an old oak tree, and your folks were headed for the mulberry bush, you'd gently turn them around and point them toward the treasure.

When they started for the maple tree, again you'd turn them around and lead them toward the oak. Try to see God as someone who's absolutely crazy about you. He wants nothing but the very best for you, his precious child.

When God prevents a relationship from working out, don't get discouraged. Instead, thank him for wanting your happiness *even more than you want it*. Continue to trust him.

Will the right guy ever come along? I wish I could answer that for you. But only God knows that secret. But you know what? Even if the right guy *doesn't* come along—even if you're single— you can still be whole and fulfilled and extremely happy in your relationship with Christ.

I am. I hope to get married someday, but right now? I'm basing my security and my fulfillment in my walk with the Lord.

Dear Susie:

I've been dating a boy from my church for six months. We've been good friends, and we really like each other. Tonight after church, he said that we should break up for a while because we're getting too involved. But we've never done anything to be ashamed of! I still love him, and I want to talk with him so I can tell him that, but I'm afraid he won't talk to me.

Tomah, WI

Break-ups hurt, don't they? They really do. And I'm sorry you're experiencing the pain of a break-up right now. I'd love to take you out for a Coke and talk it all out. Here's what I'd challenge you to think about.

Since you didn't offer any information about what you did or didn't do physically, I don't know if you were too involved or not. But you know what? That's really not the issue. If your boyfriend feels you were too involved, then you have to respect his feelings. Maybe the Lord is dealing with him about his physical involvement. I'm glad he has a tender heart. I don't know too many guys who would back off for those reasons. I admire that.

You say you still love him and want to tell him that. Could this be why he thinks you were too involved? Obviously he doesn't feel as strongly as you do. If you're already feeling like you love him, chances are he's feeling things are going waaaay too fast!

Never be the first one in a relationship to tell a guy you love him. That might scare him away. And you don't *need* to be in love during your teen years. You need to be working on good, solid friendships with the opposite sex. FRIENDSHIPS, not "in love" feelings.

Should you tell him how you feel? Absolutely not. You say he won't talk to you. Take the hint. You've been coming on too strong, and he wants out. Let him go.

Dear Susie:

My boyfriend and I have been friends forever. We grew up together, and now we're dating. He's a strong Christian and loves the Lord. Do you think at my age—sixteen—I could be falling in love with him? Some people think that's crazy.

We've both made a promise to remain sexually pure until marriage. We've also decided to take things slow. He's the best!

Madison, ME

I certainly don't think it's impossible! I hope you're rounding out your life with other things and not becoming obsessed with him. That's not healthy. But if this guy is everything you've described him to be, he sounds terrific.

What's the danger of falling in love at such a young age? You may think, *It's just a matter of time; we're going to get married.* And even though you're planning on remaining sexually pure until your wedding night, if you begin expressing your love to one another verbally, it becomes harder to maintain that pledge. Be careful.

Dear Susie:

There's a guy in my youth group who thinks all the girls are madly in love with him. We're not; we just want to be his friends, and we've told him that. What more can we do to get the message across?

Evans, IN

Unfortunately some guys just *don't* get the message. Many times a girl will simply try to be friends with a guy, and he'll misinterpret that as a come-on. But to be honest, we do the same thing sometimes, don't we? A guy will say "hi" to us or go out of his way to be nice, and we're convinced he wants to ask us out. Sometimes this whole guy/girl thing can be downright confusing!

If you've already told him and he hasn't caught the message, then you may have to use your actions to convey the message. Don't do *anything* that could be interpreted as interest in your part. You may even have to back away from being friends with him for a while. Again, that's unfortunate, but some guys just don't want to accept the truth.

PART 3
Hazards to Avoid

What should girls understand about guys?

"We need space. Don't try to smother us. If we feel like you're too possessive, we'll back off. We NEED and WANT to spend time with our other guy friends."

Jeremy, 16

What keeps you from being bored during church?

"I take notes on what's being preached. This forces me to listen more closely. Later, if I'm going through a tough time, I'll look back over my notes, and it really helps!"

Brent Caskell, 13

Do guys like to get notes from girls?

"If I like her, sure! It lets me know she's thinking about me when we're apart. But I don't enjoy getting notes from girls I don't know well. Same with phone calls. I'm an old-fashioned guy. I want to initiate the calls myself... unless it's my girlfriend or a girl I'm really good friends with."

Bryan, 18

Chapter Eight

BE CAREFUL HOW YOU STEREOTYPE

Labeling people is often detrimental.

Geek

From "dumb jock" to "computer nerd," there are labels for just about any group of people.

Some common labels or stereotypes are:

"She's just a dumb blonde."

"People who make good grades are geeks."

"A jock's brains are in his muscles."

"All Christians are fanatics."

"Real men don't cry."

 Brain Even though these statements aren't true, they can hurt people's feelings. If it's wrong to label people, why are we so quick to place stereotypes on those around us?

We can ruin our chances of establishing—or strengthening—friendships with people when we allow ourselves to believe stereotypes. When we do that, we don't allow those we know to be their individual selves.

We women do that with guys, don't we? We have our preconceived notions of what guys are like, and we forget that each guy has his own personality and character.

When establishing friendships with guys, be careful not to put them in a box. Remember, no two guys are alike. Just because *some* guys love sports, doesn't mean your next guy friend will.

Here's a terrific story, written by a friend of mine, that shows what can happen when we stereotype people.

THE ULTIMATE OF COOL

"You could go out with *any* girl in the entire school! Why would you want to go out with... with... what's her name?" grilled Bruce.

"Rebekah," volunteered Mark when Joe didn't respond.

"Yeah, that's her."

Joe shook his head, bending over to tie his Reeboks. "Lay off, guys."

"You're captain of the wrestling team. You have an image to maintain. Rebekah is not the kind of girl who has the right, uh, *look,*" Bruce continued.

Joe stood up, stomping his feet a little to straighten his pant legs. He stood in front of the mirror that was hanging in his locker and combed his hair.

"Why don't you ask Courtney out?" Mark encouraged.

"Or Karissa?" added Bruce.

Mike held up his hand and ticked off on his fingers, "Or Jamie, Michelle, or Carol. Now *those* are babes who fit the image!" He elbowed Bruce, who grinned knowingly.

"I *said* lay off," Joe said, sounding more than a little irritated at this whole conversation. "I want to go out with Rebekah."

"*Why?*" asked Bruce, amazed. "She doesn't know how to dress, doesn't know how to look you in the eye, and doesn't even know how to spell her own name."

"What's *that* supposed to mean?" Joe asked, his comb poised, his dark eyes spitting daggers in the direction of his "friends."

"Who ever heard of Rebekah spelled with a *k* and an *h?*"

"That's not even worth an answer," Joe said.

"Come on, Joe," Mark pleaded. "The name of the game is wrestling...."

"Yeah, wrestling in the back seat," snickered Bruce.

"Plenty of them willing," added Mike. "Why waste your time on Rebekah? Rebekah with a *k* and *h* won't be willing to ponder the ceiling of your car."

"You're all a bunch of jerks," Joe said, slipping his comb in his pocket. He pushed through the crowd of sweaty and showered bodies out of the locker room and into the sunshine.

He jammed his hands into his pockets and walked across the quad to the cafeteria. His brows drew together, wondering how he was going to persuade Rebekah to go out with him. He didn't understand her hesitance to speak with him... her almost antagonistic responses to him.

Balancing his loaded tray, he dodged speeding students and looked for an empty place at a table. He was so angry with his friends that he preferred to eat alone.

In the far corner of the cafeteria, two girls sat surrounded by empty places. As Joe eased his tray onto the table and himself in the chair across from Rebekah, a dark look crossed her face. "Hi, Rebekah. Hi, Julie."

Julie smiled. "Hi, Joe."

Rebekah looked down at her food, her thin, straight hair barely missing a spot in the mashed potatoes.

"I was hoping we could talk," Joe said, looking at Rebekah.

"About what?" she snapped, with fire in her eyes.

"I, uh, I'd like to get to know you better," Joe offered.

"Sure you would."

Joe looked at her as he placed cartons of milk in a line on the table. "I really would."

"Look, I'm not stupid. I've had it with you guys making a fool out of me, and I won't fall for it again." With that, Rebekah picked up her tray and walked away.

In loyalty to her friend, Julie picked up her tray and stood to follow her. But before she left, she bent down and whispered to Joe, "Don't worry, it's not just you. It's all teenage males."

"Why?"

"Later." Julie slipped him a piece of paper, then walked away without looking back.

Joe opened the paper. It had a phone number on it. He sighed, then ate his lunch alone.

That night Joe called the number Julie had given him, hoping Rebekah would answer.

Julie answered the phone. "Oh," he said, disappointed. "I thought you gave me Rebekah's number."

"Are you nuts? She'd kill me. She'd kill me if she knew I was talking to you now."

"So why *do* you want to talk to me?"

"I want to explain about Rebekah."

"So, go ahead," Joe encouraged, a little anxious and *very* curious.

"She hates guys because she thinks they're all out to hurt her."

"Why?"

"Look at her."

"I think she's cute," Joe answered.

"No, you don't. She's not cute. She's plain and simple, doesn't wear makeup, or know what to do with her limp hair. And her clothes are atrocious."

Joe was silent for a moment. "Why are you her friend if you don't like her?"

"I didn't say I don't like her," Julie said. "I'm just pointing out the facts from a male perspective. I know her from church. She's a wonderful person."

"Not all guys are alike. I happen to think she's cute. I like her smile. I like her honesty. I've heard her stand up for what she believes. She's not afraid of what the teacher or anyone else thinks. I want to get to know her better."

Julie's voice relaxed. "OK, you pass."

"Pass what?"

"My inspection. I wanted to know what you *really* wanted before I give you the scoop."

Joe smiled. "OK, so scoop it out."

"Before Rebekah went on the two-year short-term mission with her family to Guatemala, she was asked to the Sophomore Hop."

"She was a freshman then, right?"

"Yep. It was her first date ever. His name was Paul, and he was a forward on the basketball team. She bought a gorgeous dress on their limited budget, had her hair done, and mom and dad snapped pictures every time she moved. At the dance, he walked in and said, 'You're on your own.' Then he started laughing and got high-fives from all his friends. It was a joke. A dare.

"She held her head high and stayed the whole evening. But no one asked her to dance. Everyone clung in little groups, whispering, pointing, and laughing."

Joe shook his head. "No wonder she hates me. I'm just another jock."

"Ever since her family came back from Guatemala, she's been having trouble getting used to America again. I guess it's called culture shock. And bad memories have made her clam up even more."

Now he was beginning to understand. But that still didn't answer the question that was the key to this whole situation.

"How can I get her to trust me?"

"I don't know. And I'm not going to help you."

"Thanks a lot," Joe said sarcastically.

"I think you're telling the truth, but I'm not going to take the chance that someone is going to hurt her that badly again," Julie explained. "I've only known her for two months. I'm not going to risk our friendship for anyone."

Joe hung up the phone and tried to think of what he could do to convince Rebekah he wasn't like the guy who hurt her. He couldn't think of any solutions.

Two weeks passed without Joe even being able to say "hello" to Rebekah. He watched her from a distance, noticing how she smiled when she talked with the Spanish teacher or Julie. She seemed so gentle when she tutored students in the quad. How could he break through her barriers?

Every Tuesday and Thursday after wrestling practice, Joe drove his beat-up Toyota to a small brick building ten blocks from school. There, he became "Mister Joe" to a handful of the sweetest kids he'd ever known. Most had Down's Syndrome, but all of them had some sort of mental disability that prevented them from attending public school.

Joe never told anyone where he went Tuesdays and Thursdays. He didn't need the glory or ridicule. Besides, it was another image-breaker for the wrestling team's captain. He didn't feel he should have to explain to a bunch of jerks who thought they knew what life was all about why he volunteered his love and commitment to these kids.

On Thursday, Joe had three of the kids balanced on his knees. Kim, Max, and Kara all giggled as he shared a story from the Bible. His hands flew as he told the parable of the lost sheep to his delighted audience. He talked in an animated voice, using different tones for the sheep, the shepherd, and even the rocks.

"And then the rock said, 'Well, Mr. Shepherd I do believe I saw your sheep yesterday. Went by the river, he did. Might ask over there if they've seen him....'"

He sensed someone was close by, behind him. A parent maybe. Or a teacher. The room was always alive with the sounds of kids at play, learning, or singing. Joe had learned to tune it out and concentrate on the kids he was with. He continued his story without looking up.

When he finished, Kara grabbed his cheeks with her chubby hands. "Oooh, I love you, Mister Joe!" She kissed him soundly on one cheek, jumped down, and trotted off. Joe watched her and smiled.

"Joe," a soft voice called him from behind. He turned to see Rebekah standing behind him.

His face flushed and he jumped up, putting Kim and Max on the floor. "I, uh… I'm just here today, helping out. Why're you here?"

"My cousin goes here. Her mom couldn't pick her up today and asked if I'd do it." Rebekah smiled the same as she did when she talked to the Spanish teacher. "I didn't know, Joe…."

"You've got it all wrong," he said, stumbling, embarrassed, afraid he'd become the newest nerd in the school if anyone found out. "I'm just filling in for, uh, my mom," he lied.

He turned and walked away quickly, finding a group of kids spreading paint all over glossy paper with their fingers and hands. He squatted down and joined in.

Moments later, the director, with Rebekah standing beside her, walked over to where Joe was entertaining the children. "Joe, I would like to introduce you to Rebekah," she said, smirking. "She's new here and goes to your school. It would be nice if you would maybe show her around town."

Joe just stared.

The director continued, "I have two extra tickets to the Michael W. Smith concert next week. I'll give them to you if you promise to take Rebekah. Show her around, help her feel comfortable and reacquainted to this crazy environment called the United States."

"Uh," Joe mumbled, glancing at Rebekah, ready to see fire in her eyes again. Instead, he saw her gleeful smile spreading over her whole face. "Yeah, I guess I could."

"Great." The director smiled at them and returned to her duties.

Joe looked at Rebekah. "Are you sure you really want to go with a jock? You don't have to."

"As long as I'm going with Mister Joe, it will be a pleasure." With that, Rebekah took her cousin in her lap and sat at the table, dipping her fingers into the blue paint. Her eyes took on a mischievous look. "Don't worry. Your secret's safe with me."[1]

STEREOTYPES CAN KILL

It's silly for guys to think that all girls love cooking, sewing, and cleaning, isn't it? (I don't even know *how* to sew, let alone love it!) Maybe you enjoy playing tag football or jogging.

It's just as silly for us to stereotype all guys and assume they all love hunting, sports, and getting dirty. We'd live in a dull world if we didn't have talented young men who design, create, write, and sing, wouldn't we?

Remember the labels we talked about in the first part of the chapter? If directed at *you,* any one of those assumptions would hurt, wouldn't they? It's not only *unfair* to label or stereotype people, but it can actually *damage* their self-esteem.

One of the Ten Commandments given by God is "Thou shalt not kill." You may never have even thought about killing someone, but there's more than one way to break that commandment. You can "kill" a person by branding them with a false label. A detrimental stereotype can ruin someone's reputation, confidence, and friendships.

When you're tempted to label someone, or when you hear others placing someone in a stereotypical role, don't join in the game. YOU rise above it! Dare to see each person you meet as a special and unique individual... someone who's just waiting to be your friend.

1. "The Ultimate Cool" by Lissa Halls Johnson, first appeared as "Wrestling with Misconceptions," *Brio*, April 1992.

Chapter Nine

BATTLING THE JEALOUSY MONSTER

Absolutely *nothing* will turn a guy away faster than jealousy. Left unchecked, jealousy is a monster that can devour all your friendships.

Face it. No one likes to be around someone who's either getting her feelings hurt or spreading rumors because of another's good fortune. And guys notice when girls are jealous of other girls. They also notice how they handle it.

Jealousy is another hazard to avoid. Don't let it wreak havoc on your girl friendships *or* your guy friendships. The sooner you learn to be genuinely happy for the success of others, the higher quality of friendships and relationships you'll be able to establish. In fact, one who learns to be *proud* of her friends instead of *jealous* is the one others are usually drawn to. Fact of life: People are attracted to someone who isn't threatened by their success.

JEALOUSY:
The green-eyed monster.
(Or blue-eyed, or
brown-eyed, or...)

So, since jealousy is an immediate killer and a major ingredient in ruining *anything,* let's find out where *you* stand in this department. Ready? Here's a quiz to help you find out.

THE JEALOUSY QUOTIENT

1. You and Allison have made plans to hit the mall this Saturday. But on Friday night, she announces that her mom just told her that her cousin is coming in and asks if you mind if Tami comes along. From what Allison's told you in the past, you know that Tami's a head cheerleader, dates lots of guys, and is beautiful. You...

___ a. quickly make an excuse about needing to get a jump on your homework, so you can get out of the evening altogether.

___ b. say, "Ah, Allison. This was supposed to be *our* night. Can't Tami hang out with someone else till you get home?"

___ c. respond enthusiastically thinking, *the more, the better,* and suggest that the three of you grab a pizza before hitting the mall.

2. Marissa calls on Saturday afternoon squealing with delight. "Guess who just called me!" she screams. "Brad Wilson! And he wants us to go get a Coke together!" You...

___ a. say, "That's great, Marissa," with fake happiness, while clenching your teeth.

___ b. say, "Really? I can't believe it! I'm so happy for you. Want me to come over and help you pick out something to wear?"

___ c. say, "I heard he's a real jerk, Marissa."

3. At a school football game with your friends, you spot Tom, a guy you've had a major crush on for months. When you return from the concession stand with a giant pretzel and a Sprite, you

see him and your best friend giggling and sitting extremely close to each other. You...

    __ a. dump your drink on *him,* throw your pretzel at *her,* and walk away mad.

    ✓ b. cuddle next to Tom and ask him if he wants to share your pretzel.

    __ c. feel disappointed inside, but realize if he likes you, he'll eventually come around.

4. You are part of a large youth group that is going on a weekend retreat. You get assigned to the bus with teens you don't know very well, and most of them are younger than you. Your best friend gets to ride on the bus with all your other friends and the cool older guys. You...

    __ a. sit next to the window, wishing you hadn't come.

    __ b. join in with the singing and laughing, and try to get to know as many of the younger teens as possible.

    ✓ c. squint through the window trying to see all that's going on in the other bus. When you pull over at a rest stop, you grab the youth leader and insist he place you with your friend.

5. Your best friend just cut her hair. Everyone keeps telling her how great it looks. You...

    __ a. say that you thought about cutting yours too, but didn't think short styles would be popular that long.

    ✓ b. get a wavy perm.

    __ c. write her a note explaining how cute she looks.

6. You've been trying to get up the nerve to talk to Danny for three weeks. As you approach your locker, you see him talking with your younger sister. You...

    ✓ a. say, "Hi, Danny. I see you've met my little sister."

    __ b. say, "Hey, sis! Too bad you're grounded tonight and won't be able to go to the basketball game, huh?"

    __ c. say, "Hi, guys! Either of you going to the game tonight?"

7. At the school talent show tryouts, a girl younger than you is doing a great job singing. You...

__ a. try not to tap your feet, thinking, *She's not THAT good.*

✓ b. grin, tap your feet, and wish you had her talent.

__ c. tell the judges that she choked in *last* year's show.

8. You've been hinting to your boyfriend that you want a specific compact disc for your upcoming birthday. When you hear he buys the last one in the store for his cousin, you...

__ a. divert your attention to your next favorite CD.

__ b. ignore your boyfriend for a week.

✓ c. tell his cousin that you've heard some bad rumors about the group.

9. At a party, your boyfriend has talked with every girl there. You...

__ a. seek out every guy you can find while keeping an eye on your boyfriend to see if he notices.

✓ b. go in the next room and enjoy the movie everyone else is watching.

__ c. grab the snack tray and make the rounds—offering everyone seconds—so you can keep an eagle eye on his every move.

10. You and your best friend both apply for part-time jobs at your favorite clothing store. One reason you like it so much is because of the cute male employees. She's hired, but you're not. You...

✓ a. stop by on her first day and try on thirteen blouses, hoping she'll introduce you to the good-looking guys.

__ b. continue your job hunt, hoping to get hired at a nearby store so you can still drive to work together.

__ c. make an anonymous phone call to the supervisor saying that she's on probation.

11. You worked for two weeks on your history report, and you received a B. Your friend Danielle started hers two nights before it was due and got an A. You...

___ a. stay after class and ask the teacher to go through it with you, so you'll know how to improve.

✓ b. suggest to Danielle that you almost did yours on the same topic but wanted a more challenging subject.

___ c. ask her if she cheated.

12. You and Amber both tried out for the soccer team. She made it, but you didn't. You...

___ a. say, "I never really wanted to be on that dumb old soccer team, anyway."

___ b. say, "Come over after supper and we'll kick the ball around in my back yard, OK?"

✓ c. say, "I'm really much better at tennis, anyway."

SCORING

To total your score, go back and find the letter of the responses you picked. Then look at the following key and see how many points your answers are worth toward your total. Add up all the points from your answers to get your final score.

1. a=2, b=3, c=1   1

2. a=2, b=1, c=3   2

3. a=3, b=2, c=1   2

4. a=2, b=1, c=3   1

5. a=3, b=2, c=1   1

6. a=2, b=3, c=1   3

7. a=2, b=1, c=3   1

8. a=1, b=2, c=3   3

9. a=3, b=1, c=2   1

10. a=2, b=1, c=3   2

11. a=1, b=2, c=3   2

12. a=3, b=1, c=2   2

The jealousy monster (29-36 points)

If you're honest with yourself, you'll probably see that you play a lot of comparison games with your friends and classmates. Always feeling that you have to compete with the people around you will eventually drive you nuts.

Instead of being your own worst enemy, learn to love yourself and enjoy the things you *do* have going for you. Always wishing you had what everyone else has will only make you insecure. People don't enjoy being around someone who's always angry or jealous about someone else's accomplishments. Try to discover the good things about you!

Believe in yourself and those around you, and you can bring that score down!

Is it really that important? (20-28 points)

Your scores show you tend to blow things out of proportion.

Instead of pouting when your friends have good fortune, learn to be happy for them. Many times you *are* glad for them, but you don't always know how to express it. Keep working at maintaining close friendships.

You're OK (12-19 points)

Your friends trust you and generally love sharing their good news with you. They know you'll be happy *for* them and *with* them. Once in a while, you get a little envious, but you know how to handle it and what to do about it.

You've learned this valuable secret: Putting others down does not make you look better. You're a well-rounded young lady.

So... what does it all mean?

Even though this was simply a fun quiz, there's a lot of truth in it. Take your results seriously, because they could help you to make changes in some of your attitudes toward others.

Jealousy will not only hinder your friendships *now,* but it can affect the rest of your life. I know... sometimes you can't help but feel threatened by someone else's success or good fortune. That's a natural response.

But the question remains, if it's a natural response, how do we rise above it?

I'm glad you asked! I don't think it's possible to overcome something as powerful and damaging as jealousy on our own. That's where God comes in. He's ready and willing to help you overcome.

Most of the time when we're jealous of someone, it's not because we don't want to see someone else do well, but because we're worried about ourselves—we want what they have and are concerned that we may not get it. Check out what God has to say: "Don't worry about anything; instead, pray about everything; tell God your needs and don't forget to thank him for his answers" (Philippians 4:6).

God knows that this monster called jealousy can rip apart friendships, tear up churches, and damage relationships. Maybe *that's* why he lists it right alongside other sins: "Don't spend your time in wild parties and getting drunk or in adultery and lust, or fighting, *or jealousy.* But ask the Lord Jesus Christ to help you live as you should, and don't make plans to enjoy evil" (Romans 13:13-14, italics mine).

You can overcome your struggles with jealousy with God's help! Start by asking him to forgive you and help you to overcome these thoughts and attitudes. Then ask him to fill you with his incredible love for those around you.

Living a life that is free of jealousy allows you to be right with God, but it also allows you to grow in your friendships with other people. Remember... the more you love others, the more others will be attracted to you!

Chapter Ten

HOW TO DRIVE
HIM AWAY

*It doesn't take much to make
a guy lose interest.*

See Ya!

Now that we've gone one-on-one about how damaging stereotyping and jealousy can be to relationships, let's zero in on a few *other* things that can easily destroy your friendships with guys.

I believe you've read this far because you not only want to know ABOUT guys, but you want to KNOW guys themselves! In other words, you care about quality relationships, and you want to maintain the friendships you develop with the opposite sex.

Sometimes, though, without even realizing it, many girls get on a track of slowly killing the guy friendships they *do* have. You don't want to make that mistake, do you? So let's chat about five more things to watch out for. Or, in other words... DO THIS *if* you want to chase off your guy friends.

Yaketty Yak, don't snap your trap! Gossip is *always* damaging. Check out what the Bible has to say about it: "So the tongue is a small thing, but what enormous damage it can do. A great forest can be set on fire by one tiny spark. And the tongue is a flame of fire. It is full of wickedness, and poisons every part of the body. And the tongue is set on fire by hell itself, and can turn out whole lives into a blazing flame of destruction and disaster" (James 3:5-6 LB).

You'd probably never consider slipping arsenic into your guy friend's soft drink. You know the poisonous content would kill him. Yet every time you gossip about him, you're actually poisoning him.

One of the Ten Commandments is "Thou Shalt Not Kill," and most of us think, *That doesn't pertain to me. I'd never shoot anyone!* But *physical* death isn't the only way to kill someone. When you spread rumors and malicious gossip about someone, you're killing that person's reputation. Nothing destroys a friendship faster than harsh words.

Master the sprinkler-head motion. Have you ever been in this situation? You're talking to someone and trying *really* hard to be a good conversationalist. You're asking questions that demand more than a yes/no answer, and you're carefully articulating your opinions.

But as you talk with your friend, you notice that she's constantly looking past you. Whenever someone walks by, she follows him or her with her eyes like a rotating sprinkler-head. You think, *She must be searching for someone more important to talk to.* That's how it makes you feel when someone does that to you.

It hurts, doesn't it? Try to remember that when you're with a guy, he deserves your attention. Don't let him think that you're simply talking with him until someone better looking or more interesting walks by. If you do, he'll soon get the message that you are with him only out of convenience. Let your guy friends know you *genuinely* care about them by being attentive when you are together.

Name him and claim him. Nothing feels worse than being "owned" by someone. Girls who become possessive with their guy friends eventually don't *have* many guy friends.

Cara and Joey had English together and were becoming friends. On the way out of class together she said, "Call me sometime, Joey."

"OK," he said, not realizing that she meant *tonight.*

The next morning she was waiting by his locker before school started. "Why didn't you call me last night? You said you would."

"I... ah... I don't know. I got busy, I guess."

"Well, I'll see you in English class," Cara said.

It didn't take long for Cara to start being possessive with Joey. She wrote him notes and talked incessantly to him during class when he was trying to listen to the teacher. She also followed him into the cafeteria and sat next to him at lunch.

After about two weeks of this, Joey felt crowded by Cara, and began avoiding her. The problem is that she was too possessive, and Joey responded as most guys would have in this situation.

Many girls make the same mistake that Cara did. They start phoning guys a lot, seeking them out at school, and showing up where they happen to be. Like Cara, they don't know when to quit. Yes, it feels good to a guy to know that a girl is interested in him, but if he doesn't return your attention, there's a reason!

If you've sent a note to a guy or placed a phone call and he doesn't get back to you, don't make a nuisance of yourself and continue pursuing him. Guys are not big-game animals who have to be hunted down. They have feelings and pride. No guy wants to feel trapped, and the more you try to force something to happen, or the closer you try to make a guy feel toward you, the further you'll drive him away.

Mix up your signals. Keith enjoyed his friendship with Courtney, but lately he was becoming confused. She walked right past his lunch table in the cafeteria without saying a word. And it wasn't just today. She'd been doing this all week.

Yet, when they got to biology class, she acted excited about being his lab partner. She was friendly and asked him about his involvement with the school band. She even said she'd like to come to the concert next week. Outside of class, though, Courtney acted like she didn't even know Keith.

He finally got so tired of the mixed messages he was getting that he decided that pursuing a friendship with her just wasn't worth it.

In Matthew 5:33-37, Jesus talks about not making unnecessary vows. When he challenges us to make our "yes" mean "yes" and our "no" to mean "no," he's really telling us to talk straight and not give mixed messages.

Stop and evaluate the kind of verbal *and* nonverbal messages you're dishing out. Could you be confusing someone without realizing it?

Be fixing, finicky, and fussy. We girls have this nurturing instinct in us. It's how we were created, and it's what will someday make us terrific moms. But it's *not* necessarily what makes a good friend.

If there's anything a guys HATES, it's being around a girl who makes him feel as though he's being mothered. Constantly fixing his hair, fussing over a spot or stain on his shirt, or trying to straighten his collar will make him feel as though you're trying to "dress" him.

Accept your guy friend for who and what he is, and don't try to change him or make him look the way you want him to. Encourage him to be the very best he can be, but don't try to force him to change.

AND THAT'S NOT ALL . . .

This isn't the final word on what can quickly damage a once-great friendship with a guy. But the things we've just talked about *are* some of the most common mistakes teen girls make.

G U Y   T A L K

What Bugs Me about Girls

For insight on other things that frustrate guys, check out the following:

"It really bugs me when a girl flirts with another guy while she's talking to me! I guess she's just trying to get his attention, but there *are* other ways.

"If a girl wants to get to know *me*, it always helps if she'll just introduce herself and start talking. Another way to get my attention is to find out a little about me first, then use that information to start a conversation."

—Samuel, 15

"It bothers me when girls take things too seriously. I like to have fun. The whole purpose of the dating adventure is to get to know each other. When teens get too serious too fast, it only ends in hurt.

"One of my main goals is simply to be a good friend to those around me. Chances are we're not going to end up marrying the person we date in high school. When someone obsesses or worries about each dating relationship, he/she could miss out on the *friendships* God wants to bring along the way."

—Peter, 16

"It bugs me when girls are inflexible. I know a few girls who must always have their way, and if things don't go as planned, they freak.

"It also bugs me when a girl calls me over and over on the phone. That's too aggressive for me. If anything happens between a girl and me, *I* want to make the first move."

—Charlie, 16

"A lot of girls don't eat much when guys are around. I guess they assume we're going to think badly of them, or maybe they're too concerned about their appearance.

"I like it when a girl will go ahead and enjoy her meal. Any guy with character will appreciate a girl's personality and how she handles herself more than just staring at her outside package."

—Brad, 14

"It bugs me when girls spend too much time in the bathroom. I mean, sometimes it seems like they're in there *forever.* I enjoy a girl who feels confident in herself and likes the way she looks. Girls who are always pulling a mirror out of their purse and constantly primping in public are obviously worried about how people view them. Most of the time these girls look *great* just the way they are; they're worried about nothing."

—Clint, 18

"It frustrates me when girls giggle at every little thing. There's a difference between giggling and laughing. I'd rather they ask questions and actually join the conversation. When they giggle all the time, it probably means they're nervous. And when they're nervous, sometimes they talk too much. I guess sometimes it's just hard to know what to say."

—Greg, 15

"Sometimes girls jump to conclusions too quickly. A girl will say something about me to her friends, and by the time it gets back to *me,* I'm the major enemy. It bugs me when they don't talk to me first to find out what *really* happened. I think honesty is always the best policy. If a girl questions something I've said, I'll always give her the straight story. She just needs to ask."

—Dwayne, 16

"Many times a girl will look great, but she'll still say she's fat. I don't understand that. When I go out to dinner with a girl, I want to enjoy the meal *with* her instead of just watching her 'pick' at her food. That makes me feel weird—like I'm eating by myself."

—Troy, 15

"I'm really trying to be a good Christian. Sometimes it's tough. But you know what makes it *really* hard? It's when girls wear stuff that's like... revealing. It's distracting. My mom always taught me that's not cool, so it bothers me. I think I understand why they do it. It's what the world— you know, like TV—tells them they're supposed to be doing. But it really bugs me."

—Braden, 17

Mail Bag III
QUESTIONS AND ANSWERS ABOUT GUYS!

Dear Susie:

How can I let a guy know I like him without being pushy? Is it a good idea to send the message through friends?

Covington, KY

Well, that's *one* way. I really try to encourage teen girls not to be the first one to make the move, though. Instead of telling him through friends, or writing him a note, or calling him, why don't you simply try to become good friends with him? The better acquainted you become, the more comfortable he'll feel around you. If he likes you, he'll eventually let *you* know.

Dear Susie:

I'm thirteen years old and just found out that I'm pregnant. About four weeks ago, I accepted Jesus Christ as my savior. I know I've sinned by having sex outside of marriage, and I know God will forgive me, but I feel so alone.

All my friends think it's great that I'm pregnant. The biggest part of my problem is that I don't know how to tell my parents. My life is falling apart. I've even thought about committing suicide. I know God doesn't want me to do this, but it seems like the only way out.

Lansing, MI

I'm assuming your friends think it's great that you're pregnant because they're not Christians and don't understand what breaking God's law is all about.

But the truth is, getting pregnant outside of marriage is never cool. I'm so glad you know that God forgives you. He not only forgives you, but he wants to give you a brand-new start. I know you *feel* all alone, but he's right next to you feeling the hurt, loneliness, and confusion *with* you. Let him be your strength. Learn to lean on him during the next few months—you'll need him.

I'm sorry you feel like committing suicide right now. I can imagine you wanting all the hurt and confusion to go away, but suicide isn't the answer. That's not what God wants. Let him help you make the right decisions from here on out.

About telling your parents... I don't think there is an easy way to do this. Start by telling them that you know what you did was wrong and you don't want to ADD to that wrong by having an abortion. Explain that you want to give birth to the baby. They, God, and your pastor can help you decide whether to keep the baby or give it up for adoption.

The important thing for you to remember is that your life is *not* ruined! God still has exciting things in store for you. He wants the very best for you. As you continue to pray and seek his guidance, I'm confident he'll direct you.

Dear Susie:

I'm thirteen and in the seventh grade. My parents are really strict about guys. I know this is just because they love me and want to keep me safe—but they're going overboard!

I have a boyfriend right now and am going out behind their backs. I don't want to disobey them, but I'm not willing to give him up. Do you have any suggestions on how to get them to let me have a boyfriend?

Reno, NV

Well, you're not going to win any points with them by going behind their backs. Bottom line: You've *gotta* obey your parents. You don't have to agree with them, but God *commands* you to obey.

Be up front with your parents. Confess that you've gone behind their backs and that you have a boyfriend. Apologize and explain that you want them to trust you. (Of course, this may take some time, since they're just finding out they *can't* trust you!).

Tell them you want a little more space, and ask if you can start small. See if there are some things you both can agree on. In other words, can a compromise be worked out? Ask if they'll let you have guys over to the house (no, not a guy alone, not guys alone, but guys AND girls together). Ask if you can begin to do things in groups.

You may have to work at gaining their trust, but start *right now* by being honest. And if their answer is no, prove to them that you *can* be trusted by obeying them and calling it off with your boyfriend. As they watch your obedience, they'll eventually begin to trust you and give you more space.

Dear Susie:

I read in the Bible that it's wrong to have premarital sex. But if you and a guy friend are both completely undressed and in bed together—doing whatever—but NOT having intercourse, is that the same as having sex? Or is this still a sin?

Seattle, WA

What's "whatever"? You're being vague. Lying in bed is not having sex. But turn to chapter fourteen and read the chapter on sexual purity. Being sexually pure isn't just not having intercourse; it's a *lifestyle*. Yes, lying in bed naked with a guy when you're not married is a sin. That's NOT a sexually pure lifestyle.

It sounds as though you're really confused about sexual boundaries. I suggest you talk with your parents and your youth leader about establishing some clear physical guidelines for your dating life.

Dear Susie:

I want a boyfriend, but I can't narrow down which guy—of the two I like—is cuter.

Farmers Branch, NE

Hmmm. I'm not sure you're actually ready for a dating relationship yet. NO relationship should be based on something as surface as looks. How would *you* like it if a guy didn't ask you out because he thought another girl was cuter?

Spend some time with an adult who can help you gain the proper perspective on establishing good, solid male friendships based on something much deeper than physical appearance.

Dear Susie:

I'm fifteen years old and started dating this guy at church. It wasn't that good of a relationship, though. We also go to the same school, and he never even talked to me at lunch. I sent him notes and stuff, but he never sent me anything back.

We only lasted a week and a half. When we broke up, he had one of his friends come tell me he didn't want to go out any more.

At first, I hated him and wished all kinds of bad things would happen to him, but I know that's not Christlike, and now my feelings are coming back for him.

One of my older friends told me to wait and let him grow up a little. But I see him every Sunday and all during the week at school. It's hard. What should I do?

St. Charles, MO

I know it's hard. You're missing being involved in a relationship. But if the relationship wasn't that great in the first place, why are you wanting back in? See, I don't think it's really *that* relationship you're wanting. I think you just want to be with a guy. You want someone to want you.

I agree with your older friend. Give the guy the space he obviously wants and needs. Let his emotions mature. Let him discover what he really wants in a relationship. It might be that he *doesn't* want someone who's always writing him notes and trying to track him down at school.

Grab a cherry Icee and jot down all the things you've learned from this relationship. Keep these lessons in a special "dating book." Try not to make the same mistakes again, but become stronger with each guy. You sound like someone with a tender heart who wants to lavish attention on someone she cares about. And *someday* that'll probably be possible. Just not now. And just not with him.

Dear Susie:

My boyfriend just got back from juvenile hall. He was sent there on charges of armed robbery and assault. He got his ear pierced for a third time while he was there. I don't know how to tell him that I won't continue to go out with him because of the new pierce. Please help!

Carol Stream, IL

You won't go out with him because of the *new pierce?* Hmmm. I think there ought to be a few *other* reasons you no longer want to date him.

Obviously, this guy doesn't share your faith in God or your values. He's in for assault and robbery, and you're concerned about his ear? Wake up! Why are you even dating someone with this kind of lifestyle? Please rethink your reasons for dating, period. Are you going out with guys because you need attention? Because you want to feel loved? Find a healthy male role model (if you don't have a close relationship with your dad) and talk to him about your dating standards. Where can you find a male role model? What about your pastor, a favorite teacher or coach, your Sunday school teacher, a school counselor, or your youth leader? For specific guidelines in searching for a male role model, hike back to chapter two.

Dear Susie:

My boyfriend and I met in Florida while visiting our grandparents for spring break. He lives about a half hour away from me and our grandparents live next door to each other.

We started going out two days after we arrived in Florida. We really like each other, and we write letters and send pictures, but we never see each other.

*Our parents are too busy to drive us to see each other, and nei-
ther of us can get our driver's licenses for another six months. We
don't want to break up, so what can we do to strengthen our relationship and keep ourselves together?*

Burke, VA

Wow. Long-distance relationships are hard. Even though you
only live thirty minutes apart, it might as well be thirty hours,
since neither of you can drive.

I suggest you talk on the phone and write letters. There's really nothing more you *can* do, is there? Meanwhile, though, I
encourage you to become friends with other guys in your area.
You can become so obsessed with someone who's long-distance
that you miss a knight in shining armor who could be living in
the next block.

PART 4
Let's Talk Physical

Are teen guys scared of anything?

"We're afraid of death, but most guys try not to show that. There's so much violence on the streets, you can't help but wonder about being killed or dying young.

"We're also afraid of divorce. Seems like everyone's parents are doing it. And it's scary, because you may feel closer to your mom than your dad, yet he might be the one who gets custody. Or you may even have to make a choice—and that's pretty frightening! How can a teen choose between his parents?"

Scott, 15

What's the biggest difference between guys and girls?

"Girls tend to get more intimate with their friends, whereas guys usually keep things surface between each other. Girls enjoy talking about the feelings; guys talk about events—like last night's game. Girls care about all the details; guys just want the facts."

Chris Bell, 16

Chapter Eleven
WORTH THE WAIT!

*Ever feel like you're the only one in the whole
world who's saving herself for marriage?
Believe me, you're not!*

A few weeks before her thirteenth birthday, Shauna Menefee started dropping hints about what she wanted. Actually, "hints" doesn't really describe what she did, which was simply tell her parents what she wanted: "A ring would be really cool."

They not only picked up her "hint" but drove her to the jewelry store and let *her* pick out the ring!

"It was really fun," Shauna remembers. "We looked at several, but I kept coming back to this pretty gold one. It had a heart in the middle that really caught my eye."

Shauna's parents purchased the ring, wrapped it, and kept it hidden for two weeks. Right before her birthday, her dad surprised her.

"Shauna, your thirteenth birthday is really special. Your mom and I want to treat you to a nice dinner at a classy restaurant," he said. "We'll all dress up and make a memory we'll never forget."

The big day finally arrived, and after Shauna was presented with a beautiful corsage, she and her parents headed out for an evening of fine dining.

"After we placed our dinner order, my mom pulled out several birthday gifts," Shauna said. "I unwrapped a new belt, some hair bows, a book I had been wanting... but no ring."

Their steaks arrived, and as they were enjoying the meal, her dad started talking about the ring.

"Shauna, you picked out a beautiful ring for your thirteenth birthday. And though you didn't know this, it's a very *special* ring."

"We're going to call it a chastity ring," her mom said.

"In the next few years you'll date a variety of young men," her dad continued. "And your mom and I want you to uphold the dating standards we've helped you establish. We expect you to maintain your sexual purity until marriage."

"Shauna," her mom said, "let this ring be a symbol of your virginity. It will represent your commitment to God to remain abstinent until you're married."

As Shauna opened the beautifully wrapped package, she couldn't help but feel the depth and seriousness of the gift.

"I had already decided to maintain my sexual purity," she recalls. "I'm a Christian—it's not an option. I'm determined to follow God's will for my life.

"But as I slipped this special ring on my finger, it deepened my heart's desire to become all that God wants me to be."

Shauna's sixteen years old now. "When I'm out with a guy," she said, "and he reaches for my hand, I feel my ring against his flesh, and that's a pretty powerful reminder of my commitment.

"And when I catch myself daydreaming in class, I start fiddling with my ring—you know—twisting it round and round. And I smile deep inside, knowing that someday I'll present this very ring to my husband on our wedding night as a symbol of the most important gift I can give him—my virginity.

"I realize I may fall in and out of love several times before I finally commit to the man God wants me to marry," she said. "This ring is not just a symbol of virginity; it's also a reminder not to do *anything* on a date that I'll regret. So my ring is a constant reminder to take everything that happens during a date seriously."

IS EVERYBODY DOING IT?

It seems like we're bombarded with messages of sexual freedom... ads, TV, movies. But really, is *everyone* doing it? Shauna sure doesn't think so.

"I realize just by watching the news that lots of young people are involved in sexual relationships," Shauna says. "The pregnancy rate for unwed teen moms continues to skyrocket, as do sexually transmitted diseases.

"But to say 'everybody's doing it' just isn't real life. *I'm* not doing it. My closest friends aren't doing it. NOT EVERYONE IS DOING IT! And to fall for that lie is just plain stupid. God has a much higher calling on our lives."

WHAT ABOUT YOU?

Shauna is a young lady who has set very high standards for herself, standards she is committed to living up to. She, like many other young people, has decided that no matter what our culture says, she will wait until God says "yes" to sex. And that time will only be *after* she has been permanently bonded to a man in a marriage relationship.

What about *you?* Are you determined to wait? Then make that commitment—to God, to your parents, and to yourself.

It's not *necessary* that you have a physical reminder (like a ring) to keep your commitment fresh. Your promise to God is the most important factor. But if you *do* want a physical reminder, there are things other than a ring that you can use.

For example, many parents present their sons and daughters with gold key chains or necklaces to serve as chastity reminders.

??? Or how about the Love Pendant? It's a beautiful golden necklace with three question marks, symbolizing "Am I being true to God? To my parents? To myself?" You can order one for approximately $20 from the Josh McDowell ministry; call 1-800-222-5674.

I'm often asked by young ladies how they can get their parents to give them a chastity symbol. These girls deeply desire to make a commitment to themselves and to God to remain pure until marriage, and they want their parents to take a part in that commitment.

I recommend that you start by talking with your mom and dad about your desire to follow God's will for your life, and tell them you want to keep your virginity until marriage.

Explain what you've read (or show them this book) and ask them if they would consider giving you a chastity symbol as a special gift.

Then, once you get your special ring, necklace, key chain, watch, or whatever it is, dare to wear it to school and talk openly about your decision to remain sexually pure.

But above all, remember it's not the *physical* item that's important. Rather, it's your *spiritual* commitment to your heavenly Father. Your chastity symbol is just a reminder of what you have purposed in your heart. Without that commitment, that symbol doesn't mean anything. On the other hand, your commitment means everything, even without a symbol.

COMMITMENT TO PURITY

There's no way around it—God commands that we save his beautiful gift of sex until marriage. If you're willing to follow his plan for your life and commit to saving yourself for your future mate, you can do something about it right now!

How about signing the "True Love Waits" commitment pledge below? Maybe you've *already* made a promise to remain pure. Would you like to reiterate that decision right now? If you're willing, with God's strength, to follow HIS ideal for sex—within marriage—instead of the world's warped view, then I challenge you to offer him this prayer and sign the pledge below.

> *Dear Father,*
>
> *I realize that you're the One who invented sex. Therefore, it only makes sense that you'd know how and where it will be most beneficial. I understand that you created this wonderful union between a man and woman to remain in the confinement of marriage. I'm pledging my sexuality to you, right now. I believe with your strength I can remain sexually pure until the day that you bring a lifetime mate into my life. Amen.*

> Believing that *true love waits,* I make a commitment to God, myself, my family, those I date, my future mate, and my future children to be sexually pure until the day I enter marriage.

_____*Stacey Binkewitz*_____   *5-15-97*
(signed)   (date)

Now that you've prayed this prayer and signed this pledge, it's important to remember that you've made a *commitment* before God to remain pure.

As you honor this pledge, so will God. It's his will that you keep yourself pure, and his Word promises that he rewards those who seek to please him.

BUT WHAT IF...

But maybe you have already lost your virginity. If so, you may feel as if you have nothing left to offer your future husband. But that's just not true! Remember, when you seek God's forgiveness, he not only forgives, but he heals and restores.

For more on this, read the following letter I received from a young lady who had lost her virginity *and* my response to her:

Dear Susie:

I feel I have betrayed God, my family, and my friends. I have slept with two guys, and I'm only thirteen. My parents are divorced, but I see my dad and his new wife on weekends. Please give me some guidance and tell me what to do!

Toledo, OH

Anytime we go against God's laws, we feel guilty. That's the whole purpose of having a conscience. God placed it within us to help keep us from doing what is wrong in his sight.

The first thing I suggest you do is go to God right now and ask forgiveness. In a second, I'll give you a prayer you can read to God. But before we do that, let's talk about *why* you've slept with two different guys at your young age.

Since you mentioned that your parents have split and your dad remarried, I'm wondering if you're subconsciously trying to get his attention. Or could it be that you're not getting enough love and affirmation from him, so you're seeking it through sex? (Please refer back to chapter two for some helpful information for girls without a father figure in their lives.)

Or it *could* be you've had sex because you don't know how to say "no." It feels good to have a guy pay special attention to you, and when he starts putting the moves on, you don't know how to stop him. Try this: "I like being with you, but I'm not ready for sex. I want to save myself for marriage." Any guy who continues to pressure you after a statement like that is a good candidate for date rape.

The important thing for you to focus on now is your future. You can start over and determine to maintain your purity until marriage. Wouldn't it be great to save yourself from this point on for your husband and him only? You can! God can supply you with the strength you need to say "no" to compromising situations.

One more thing before we pray: DON'T LET YOURSELF END UP IN A QUESTIONABLE SITUATION! Since you've had sex with two different guys, it's obvious that you've been alone with these guys. Stay in group situations. Refuse to accompany guys to secluded areas. You know your weaknesses, so don't allow yourself to be alone with a guy in a place where you could get into a questionable situation.

Now, pray.

Dear God, I am so sorry for giving away my virginity. I realize I have gone against your will, and I'm seeking your forgiveness.

Please wipe my slate clean and give me a brand-new start. I want to be all you created me to be, therefore, I'm pledging from this point on to save myself for my future husband.

I know I can't do this in my own strength. Please fill me with the power and wisdom I need to keep this commitment. Thank you for your forgiveness. Thanks for choosing to forget my sin. I'm so glad you're giving me a fresh start.

Help me to be more selective of whom I date. And help me to consciously think about my dates. I need to remember not to set myself up and to stay away from compromising situations. I love You, Father. Amen.

As a symbol of your new commitment, I encourage you to sign the "True Love Waits" card. Let it be a constant reminder that God wants to help you remain sexually pure until your wedding night.

Dear Susie:

I'm a virgin, and I know that sex is wrong outside of marriage, but what if you do have sex? How will you be cleansed besides asking for forgiveness?

Puyallup, WA

I'm not sure what you mean by being "cleansed besides asking for forgiveness." God can truly wipe your slate clean. The Bible tells us that he not only forgives, but he also chooses to forget! You can commit your virginity and sexual purity to him once again. This is sometimes referred to as "secondary virginity."

Though one can't actually go back and remove the fact that she has been physically involved with a man, she *can* rest in the fact that through forgiveness, God now sees her as a virgin. Like the woman caught in adultery, he says, "Go and sin no more."

Chapter Twelve
STOLEN

Aimee and Eric were in love... but he had a secret.

In chapter eleven, we talked about the commitment to remain sexually pure before marriage. We talked about the value God places on that commitment and the seriousness with which you should approach it.

The question that often arises, though, is "why?" Why does God want us to abstain from sex outside of marriage? Why is it set up so that sex outside of marriage is so damaging, so emotionally devastating?

God has many reasons for his commands to remain sexually pure. Some of them we can't see, feel, hear, or touch in this life. But some of them are all too obvious in our age.

Other than your decision to become a Christian, your commitment to sexual purity is the most important decision you'll ever make! To find out what can happen *without* this commitment check out the following story:

Dear Missy...

It's hard to believe that my "baby" sister is turning thirteen! I'm sorry I won't be home for your birthday, but I've got finals and my college professors are ruthless.

Missy, I wish we could have one of our "long talks," because there's so much I'd like to say to you about being a teenager.

I'm going to share something very personal, very painful—in hopes that when you fall in love, things will be different. It started last fall, when I first left home....

I didn't plan to meet him on my first day of college. I had other things on my mind. I needed to crash an 8 A.M. English class that I didn't get on my schedule.

When I rushed into the classroom and couldn't find an empty seat, I knew I wasn't the only student with this dilemma. I paused in the doorway, trying to decide what to do. I could join those who stood against the back wall, or maybe I should turn around, run out the door, and forget this whole college thing.

That's when he got up from his aisle seat and motioned me into it. He did it so naturally and with such confidence that I didn't think twice about refusing. I gratefully melted into the chair and tried to focus on what the professor said. I took precise notes on the requirements for passing English 101.

By the end of class my mind had cleared, and I wanted to thank the cute guy in the gray-blue sweater. But when I stood and looked around, he was gone. I had a sinking feeling, like I'd just missed my only chance to meet the most wonderful person in the world. So I sat back down.

While I sat there, I prayed. I always talk things over with the Lord, especially when I'm feeling confused and insecure, which is most of the time. I didn't pray out loud or anything, just talked to him in my mind.

First I thanked him for working it out so I could sit down before my knees buckled and my courage gave way to panic. I also thanked him for that thoughtful guy and asked for the chance to see him again. (I sure didn't know what I was asking for.)

When I finally left the empty room I nearly ran into that gray-blue sweater. I looked up, way up.... Being five-foot-one, I'm used to that sort of thing. A pair of clear blue eyes met mine, making me forget what I wanted to say. He stayed calm and said, "Hi. I'm Eric, what's your name?" And that's how it all began.

I knew that since I chose to attend a Christian college, chances were great that Eric was a Christian, but the chances of him being a *great* Christian were one in a million. Eric was one in a million. He took me to church the next Sunday and, although he'd only known the Lord two years, his maturity and depth of understanding left me yearning to follow his example.

We spent a lot of time together that first semester. And in between chocolate milk shakes, heart-to-heart talks, and thunderous laughter, I decided I loved him.

No matter that he'd made no attempt to hold my hand or talk about "forever." I knew he cared for and enjoyed being with me as much as I did him. I talked it over with my roommate, Sara.

"You know, Sara" I began, "I really respect Eric because he's never tried to kiss me."

"You respect him?" she asked, sitting up on her bed with interest shining in her eyes.

"Of course I do."

"Well," she said slowly, "I *did* hear of this couple, and the first time he ever kissed her was when he proposed. Now, that's self-control!"

"Bet that was some kiss!"

"Aimee," Sara said, leaning forward, "do you think Eric is waiting until he's ready to propose?"

I felt my face get hot. "I didn't say we're going to get married," I stated, even though I'd secretly thought it. "But, I think he'd make a wonderful husband."

Sara's eyes grew wide at my bold expression. Then her excitement traveled down to her feet, and she jumped up from her bed. "Oh, Aimee!" she exclaimed. "Do you mean it? Do you love him?"

With my nod I admitted to Sara that I did love Eric.

"In that case," she said with determination, "you have to get his interest. Starting out as friends is great, but it's time for this relationship to blossom."

Sara said it with the flourish of any committed drama major.

"Maybe he just needs time," I suggested.

"No way. He needs encouragement."

"Encouragement?"

"Yes. Little hints, like walking close to him and saying, 'It sure is cold out here. Wish I'd brought a sweater' or . . ." Sara paused for a moment, biting her bottom lip. "I know! How about, 'Ouch! Eric, I've hurt my ankle. You'll have to carry me to my dorm.'"

I rolled my eyes as Sara limped dramatically around our room.

"And," Sara concluded, straightening up with one finger raised skyward, "if all else fails—pray like crazy!"

I did pray. Well, I told God everything I felt and asked for what I wanted. I didn't listen much. Perhaps if I had... well I didn't.

After Christmas and Easter and months of hinting, I felt desperate. Each time I saw Eric and every moment we spent together made me love him more. His gentle sincere ways and honest style made me certain that he was the one for me. So, two weeks before summer vacation, I gathered all my courage together to tell him how I felt.

We walked through the massive redwood trees that grew behind our school. "You know," Eric said, "this small forest, this spot of untouched nature, is what convinced me to come to this college."

"I love it too," I said, while thinking, *I love you.*

"Trees are incredible, Aimee." Eric stopped and looked up through the branches of a towering redwood. Far above, the sky lay in its bright blue cloak. "They lift their branches toward heaven and silently give praise to God. They do exactly what God created them to do, and that brings him glory. He has surrounded us with beauty."

As I gazed through those branches, considering Eric's words, I felt his intent look upon me. I met admiration in those clear blue eyes.

"God has surrounded my life with beauty, through you, Aimee."

My heart began to skip and jump and pump and pound. I felt sure this was the moment.

His words came softly, sincerely. "You are my best friend. No one listens to and understands me like you do. And you're fun to be with. I can't imagine what life would have been like this year without you."

"I feel the same way, Eric," I said. "But what about this summer?"

"You know I'm going to visit my missionary friends in South America."

"But I'll miss you so much," I protested.

"I'll miss you too, Aimee."

"Eric, I love you."

"And I love you."

He said it. I heard him say it. So why wasn't I in his arms? Why didn't he *act* like he loved me?

"Eric," I tried again, "I will *always* love you. I want to always love you."

"No, Aimee. It can't be like that."

"But you said you loved me!"

"I do, and that's why…"

"Why what?" I demanded. "Either you love me or you don't. I'm in love with you."

His eyes were full of tears. In a desperate motion he grabbed me and pulled me close to his heaving chest. Great wrenching sobs came from deep within him, consuming my joy, filling me with dread.

"If I'd only known then," his voice trembled. "If I'd only known the price I'd have to pay."

I cried too, feeling confused and frightened. "What are you saying, Eric? What do you mean?"

Slowly, after moments that lasted lifetimes, he began to explain. He held my shoulders, looking down at me.

"My precious Aimee. I *do* love you. You must believe me. But we can't ever get married. Oh, I wish things were different. If I could turn back time..."

"Are you already married?" I guessed, desperate for an explanation.

"No. But there have been others in my life—many others."

"That doesn't matter to me. When you became a Christian, you became a new creation! God's forgiven all your past sins. Don't you believe that?"

"I stake my life on it."

"Then what's the problem?"

"Oh, Aimee." He cried again, and his sorrow washed over me in great waves of anguish. "Before I knew Christ, I lived differently. I was a good student, a good athlete, and a good jock. Being selfish, I tried to get into bed with as many girls as I could. Some I didn't even know."

"Eric," I said, looking directly into his eyes. "Listen to me. That doesn't matter. We'll put that behind us. We'll ask God to take away those memories."

"No, Aimee."

"Yes!" I nearly shouted it. I would not lose him or our chance at happiness. "I'll take you just as you are. I love you, Eric."

"Aimee," he said in a whisper, "Satan is a robber and a thief. He has stolen you from me with a lie. He told me I could have it all, but all I really have is AIDS."

Nothing could have prepared me for his announcement... *nothing!* Time stood still, and the world whirled around me.

AIDS. It robbed me of my future with Eric. It would eventually rob him of life.

I never saw Eric again after our good-bye in early June.

Before he boarded the plane, I kissed his face and promised to write. As his plane disappeared into the clouds, so did the dreams of the life we could have shared. He got malaria while in South America. With a compromised immune system, he never recovered.

But, little sister, I'm planning to meet him again. Yes, one day we'll meet again.

Missy, may your teen years be full of the kind of fun that leads to a lifetime of joy. Happy birthday! I love you.

Much love, from your "older but wiser" sister,
Aimee[1]

1. "Stolen" by Sue Cameron first appeared in *Brio* in March 1991.

Chapter Thirteen
A Promise for Purity

*A promise is a promise is a promise.
But a commitment? Well, that
lasts forever!*

You've made a pledge to save yourself for marriage, but you're wondering if you'll really have the strength and discipline to *keep* that commitment. *After all,* you think, *how do I know how I'll react when the pressure is on?*

Here's the good news: God wants your success in maintaining your pledge to purity *even more than you do!* He's committed to helping you remain sexually pure. Since you both want victory, let's take a quick peek at seven ways you can be a success in keeping your promise. And just to make it easy, let's spell out the word SUCCESS, OK?

A S.U.C.C.E.S.S.ful COMMITMENT

S. **Start now.** If you haven't made a commitment to sexual purity, begin right now. Flip back to page 125 and sign the "True Love Waits" pledge card. Tell some important people in your life about your commitment. Start with your parents. By sharing this news, you're allowing yourself to be accountable to those around you. They can play an important role in helping you keep your pledge.

Ask your parents to join with you in your pledge. They can encourage you to maintain *your* promise by supporting you with a holy lifestyle. Ask them to commit to the following pledge:

Parent/Adult Pledge

Believing that true love waits, I pledge to God, my child, and our youth that I will pray for them and support them in every way I can as they make this important decision to remain sexually pure from now until they enter marriage. Also, I pledge to model sexual purity in my own life.

_____ _____

(signed)   *(date)*

_____ _____

(signed)   *(date)*

U. **Understand that you can't get comfortable.** Refuse to let down your guard. If you become comfortable in questionable situations, it won't be long until your conscience becomes hardened. When *this* happens, it won't bother you to do things you wouldn't have done in the past.

For example, let's say you've established a dating guideline with your parents that says you're not to be alone with a guy in his house or your house. If you compromise on this rule and allow yourself to become comfortable being alone with him behind the church or in the storage shed on school property, you're still breaking the rules. You're just going about it differently.

When you allow yourself to become comfortable rationalizing your established guidelines, chances are it's only a matter of time until you forego your entire pledge.

C₀ Clarify your boundaries. Set specific physical guidelines that you won't cross. (For instance, "I'll never lie on the floor with a guy and watch TV" or "I'll always kiss standing up" or "I'll never do anything below the neck.") Make a list of what you feel is off limits. By writing it down on paper, you're solidifying the seriousness of your commitment.

Be honest and up front about your beliefs. If the guy who's asked you out doesn't respect them or doesn't really want to hear them, call off the date.

C₀ Create your own success story. When dating, *plan* to do it right. Part of being successful at keeping your promise to remain pure is careful planning. So take time to think about the entire evening. Leave no room to blow it.

How do you do this? Well, let's say you have a 12:30 curfew. If you're going to a basketball game then to get pizza, and it's 11:30 when you're finished, what are you going to do with that extra hour? Make specific plans ahead of time. There are tons of ways you can fill time in fun and creative ways. Go the airport and watch planes arrive and depart; go home early and make popcorn; find a phone and call all your friends. (For more information on planning really fun dates, go to your local bookstore and order a copy of *258 Great Dates While You Wait* by Susie Shellenberger and Greg Johnson, Broadman & Holman publishers.)

Don't set yourself up! By refusing to allow yourself to be in questionable situations, you're guarding your promise.

E. **Exemplify purity.** Remember, it's not simply your *virginity* you're guarding, it's your *lifestyle*. (For more on a pure lifestyle, see chapter fifteen.) Don't give away your affection too quickly. In other words, just because you've had a fun evening with a guy isn't a good enough reason to give him a good-night kiss. Wait until you're with someone you feel really deeply about—someone to whom you're committing a part of your heart.

S. **Seek other Christians.** When forming dating relationships, look for people who share your beliefs, values, and morality. The best relationships are those with common ground. What values do you share in common? Do you both have a personal, growing relationship with Jesus Christ? Are you both involved in church?

If you don't go to PG-13 movies, why go out with someone who does? If your parents don't allow you to go to dances, then don't form a close dating relationship with a guy who'll try to pressure you into going.

In every dating relationship, you'll either grow closer to Christ or further away from him. No one stays still. Choose to date guys who will enhance, not take away from, your walk with God.

S. **Stand up to the flak.** Anything worthwhile isn't easy, is it? There's usually a price involved when you're striving for high goals. It will hurt when people give you a hard time about your commitment to purity. They may feel uncomfortable with your zeal to be all God calls you to be. They won't understand your values and your convictions. But that's OK. Keep your head high and your shoulders straight, and know that God will provide the strength you need to live a holy lifestyle.

Sadly, you may even receive persecution for your beliefs from other Christians. We *expect* non-Christians to give us a hard time, don't we? After all, they're not living for purity. But it *really* hurts when our *Christian* friends give us flak for our convictions!

Too often, people in the church are quick to cut one another down and make fun of values and decisions. Don't be one of those people! God has a much higher calling on your life. Determine to be a young lady who refuses to question another person's value system. Instead, affirm and compliment those around you. That's what the body of Christ is all about—reaching out in love and walking together.

MORE THAN A SLIP OF PAPER

God is calling you to much more than simply signing a pledge card. He's asking you to make a lifetime commitment to being radically obedient to his will. Sexual purity affects your entire lifestyle. If you're serious about maintaining your purity until marriage (and I believe you are if you signed the pledge card), then you'll be willing to take a look at every area in your life that's touched by your sexuality.

The media are probably the worst for tearing apart your commitment to purity. Shows like "Melrose Place," "Beverly Hills 90210," "Models, Inc.," "Married With Children," and even "Seinfeld" do absolutely *Check out 2 Timothy 2:22* nothing to encourage values or purity. Even though Tori Spelling's character, Donna, from "Beverly Hills 90210," has remained a virgin throughout the TV series, her physical involvement with the guys she dates on the show is anything *but* pure!

The movies and music don't offer much help, either. Quentin Tarantino, director of the ultra-violent film *Pulp Fiction,* said this to *Rolling Stone* magazine on November 3, 1994: "I'm not interested in making a cartoon. I'm interested in making the violence real."

And check out what Jaye Davidson, an openly gay actor who appeared in *The Crying Game* and *Stargate,* had to say in the November 1994 issue of *Interview:* "Jesus isn't bothered by my tattoos or what I'm doing in bed. I'm sure he has other stuff to worry about."

A few years ago, our youth culture department here at Focus on the Family did a study on 2 Live Crew's *Nasty as They Wanna Be Part II* album. Their discovery was startling. Here's what they came up with from that *one* album: 227 uses of the F-word, 265 references to male or female genitals, eighty-six references to oral sex, more than three hundred uses of vulgarity and much, much more that I don't even feel comfortable printing here.

Refusing to listen to such garbage is a wise decision. But not listening to that and deciding not to date a guy who fills his mind with that kind of trash is even wiser.

Think about it: If you've decided to guard your mind and heart by being selective of what you see and hear, would you really want to trust yourself alone in a car with a guy who's into that kind of entertainment? One thing, and one thing only, will be on his mind: How much physical action can he get from you?

KEEP UP YOUR GUARD!

Signing a pledge card to maintain your sexual purity is the first step, but keeping that commitment requires action! Be aware of the negative influences around you that are fighting to steal your promise. Avoid movies that are sexually suggestive, flaunt cursing, or promote violence. Radical obedience costs a lot, but that's what God requires in order to give you the most fulfilling life imaginable.

Remember, he's the one who created you! You can trust him to help you guard yourself against the things that would keep you from becoming all he wants you to be.

Here's your ammunition. Memorize it!

"Keep a close watch on all you do and think. Stay true to what is right and God will bless you and use you to help others" (1 Timothy 4:16).

Here's a Scripture verse that we'll personalize for you. Memorize it, remembering to put your name in!

"(Insert your name), you are God's man (woman). Run from all these evil things and work instead at what is right and good, learning to trust him and love others, and to be patient and gentle" (1 Timothy 6:11).

"Run from anything that gives you the evil thoughts that young men (and women) often have, but stay close to anything that makes you want to do right" (2 Timothy 2:22).

How can we get more guys involved in "See You at the Pole"?

"We need to talk it up more. I stood at my school's flagpole last year to pray, but I stood alone. Kids made fun of me, and I was nervous, but I believed in what I was doing. God *needs* us to take a stand. And when we do, he strengthens us to *keep standing*."

Scott, 15

Chapter Fourteen
WHAT IS SEXUAL PURITY?

More than something you DO, purity is something you ARE!

The vast majority of the letters I receive are from girls with questions about guys and how they relate to them. And many of *those* letters are asking me just how far someone can go physically and still consider themselves sexually pure.

Just about any Christian knows that sexual intercourse outside of marriage is a sin. But what many teens are confused about is just what they *can* do in their dating relationships. Unfortunately, what many teens don't seem to realize is that sexual purity involves a lot more than simply being a technical virgin.

WHAT IS IT?

Many people who brag about being a virgin on their wedding days are not *really* sexually pure. You see, sexual purity involves a lot more than intercourse. It involves much more than NOT doing something.

Sexual purity involves our entire lifestyle. As we discussed in the previous chapter, the movies we watch and the music we listen to can affect our sexual commitment. But that's not all! How we act on dates and even our physical and emotional involvement with the opposite sex is a part of sexual purity.

Sadly, many people—including some of your friends, no doubt—believe that as long as they don't have intercourse, they're still sexually pure. They believe they can get as close to intercourse as possible without "going all the way" and still be OK.

My question to young people who do that is, *OK for what?* For claiming that they're pure? No way. For being clean in God's eyes? Sorry! For not doing emotional damage to the guy or girl they're with? Guess again!

Again, sexual purity is much more than a simple decision not to have intercourse. Real sexual purity is a way of life. It involves making decisions to live a life of integrity. It involves asking God to help you be a godly example to those around you.

I recently met Charity Allen, who as a senior in high school stood alone when many people would have caved in. Let me tell you the story she told me. I think you'll be encouraged and challenged by her decision to make her entire lifestyle reflect sexual purity.

LIVING IN ANOTHER WORLD

Seventeen-year-old Charity Allen was conjugating verbs in Spanish class at the Los Angeles High School for the Performing Arts, when the teacher's instructions were interrupted by a sharp tapping on the door. And without waiting for anyone to answer, the music teacher rushed in.

"I have... to talk... with Charity," he said, still trying to catch his breath after running across campus.

Charity got permission to leave class. Before she even has a chance to ask questions, her music teacher screamed, "I have the break of a lifetime for you! This could be *it*."

Charity listened eagerly while he explained that NBC casting just called. "The day-

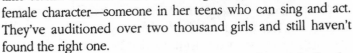

time drama 'Another World' is looking for a new female character—someone in her teens who can sing and act. They've auditioned over two thousand girls and still haven't found the right one.

"They want to know if we have anyone who's right for the part. It's YOU, Charity! *This* is going to be your big break!"

"My head was swimming," she remembers. "Anyone pursuing a career in music or acting dreams of a moment like that."

Once inside her teacher's office, she pulled out a chair and sat down. "Tell me more," Charity said.

Her teacher glowed. "'Another World' wants to attract the teen crowd. To do that, they've decided to create a new teen idol.

"NBC casting has auditioned girls all over New York and throughout Southern California. But they just haven't met YOU, Charity!"

"It sounds exciting," she said, "but... a soap opera?"

"This character is going to be an immediate star written right into the script. *Thousands* of girls all over American would die for this part," he said.

"My teacher believed *so much* in me," Charity remembers. "Seeing *his* confidence made me wonder if this was really going to be my break.

"He called NBC casting and told them he'd found their actress. I was excited, but I was also leery. When you live in the Hollywood area, you learn not to get your hopes up. The city is *filled* with hype and dreams.

"I was also skeptical," Charity told me, "because the part was for a daytime drama. My parents don't approve of soaps. We're not allowed to *watch* them. And I was going to *audition* for one? I had lots of questions."

But there wasn't time for questions. The producers were ready to move!

The producers of "Another World" faxed a script to Charity's music teacher and scheduled an audition that weekend!

"This weekend?" Charity said. "I can't. I leave *tomorrow* for Easter vacation." And this wasn't just another spring break. It was Easter in Hawaii!

Charity had a friend whose family vacationed on the island every year. Her friend was tired of just tagging along with her parents, so they decided to let her invite Charity.

"But it was more than just an invitation," Charity said. "I was being *paid* to go! They didn't want to deprive me of the baby-sitting money I would've made during spring break, so they made an offer I couldn't refuse.

"My teacher was insistent, though. He handed me the script, and we immediately headed to the casting office!

"It was really hectic. I was memorizing five pages of lines— plus the history of my character—on the way there!

So began the audition. Charity read her lines with the chair-woman of NBC casting. After several readings, the director sat down, placed her script on the big mahogany desk and smiled.

"I'm impressed," she said. "I'm *very* impressed."

Charity watched the director get up, walk around the desk and sit on its edge.

"Your life is going to change, Charity. How do you feel about moving to New York?"

Charity didn't quite catch on, so she just sat there, staring at her.

The director continued. "We'll move you in two weeks. All your expenses will be paid. You'll have your own house in Manhattan."

"Manhattan?" Charity asked.

"That's right," the director continued. "We'll also provide you with a personal tutor, so you can finish your senior year of high school."

"Manhattan, New York?" Charity asked again, still staring wide-eyed at the casting director.

"You'll also have a housekeeper, so you won't have to worry about housework and cleaning. And you can forget about subways and congested traffic."

"Why?" Charity said. "Isn't that what New York's all about?"

"Not for you. You'll have your own private chauffeured limousine."

"Everything was happening so quickly," Charity told me. "Get this: My family lives in a two-bedroom mobile home! There are four of us kids in one room; my parents and baby sister share the other. So, hearing about a *real* house really caught my attention.

"Even though I'm a high school senior, I still don't have my driver's license. It's not that I don't want it; we just can't afford the insurance.

"And this woman is telling me I'll have my own limo? I felt like Cinderella getting ready for the ball. It sounded like they were promising me the whole world!

"The fireworks went off in my head. I finally realized I'd gotten the part!"

But with that realization came the fear of having to leave her family.

"It sounds wonderful," Charity told the director. "But I'm seventeen years old. I'm not ready to leave my family yet."

The director stared at her soon-to-be star. "You don't get it, do you?"

Charity shifted her weight and leaned forward. "What do you mean?"

"I mean, you're going to be a *star!* You'll have it *all*. Charity, we'll move your family to New York *with* you. You'll all be living together with everything you want in your own Manhattan house!"

"I gotta call mom," she said.

Once Cindy Allen got on the phone, she thanked the head of NBC casting for making her daughter such a gracious offer. But she was quick to explain the family's situation.

"My husband's a schoolteacher. I don't know if he could find a teaching job in New York. We have five children. Frankly, we just don't have the money to survive in Manhattan."

"I don't think you understand, Mrs. Allen," the director began. "We're hiring Charity as an immediate *star.* Her salary alone will be more than enough for your entire family."

Now, *Cindy's* thoughts began to swirl. More than enough? *Just how much money are we talking about here?*

Charity could be making up to twenty thousand dollars a week. *Yep. That should cover living expenses.*

The executive continued. "Mrs. Allen, *I've* looked all over L.A., and *they've* searched New York, and CHARITY is exactly what we want for this character. I'm going to call the producers immediately and tell them I've found the person we've been looking for."

ANY QUESTIONS?

Whew! A *lot* had happened since earlier that morning when Charity had fought off brothers, sisters, and parents for the bathroom. It was incredibly exciting, yet Charity couldn't help but voice her doubts.

"I'm not really a soap watcher," she explained. "I've seen a few but am not a fan. So, I'm curious… what's the agenda for my character?"

The director looked up from her desk. "What do you mean, *agenda?*"

"I'll be honest with you," Charity explained. "I have standards for myself that I *will* be true to. If your agenda for this character is opposite that, I'll have to let this opportunity go."

The director was all ears. "What kind of standards?"

Charity scooted her chair right up to the big desk and leaned forward.

"I'm a Christian. God is *absolutely* number one in my life. Now, that means a lot of things, but here are a few of the specifics.

"I will not be involved in intimate love scenes. In my *personal* life, I won't have sex until I'm married. Therefore, I will not imitate lovemaking in my *professional* life. Not for me.

"And I'll never use God's name in vain. Nor will I swear. I also refuse to act in any situation where I'm promoting drug use. These things are *very* important to me, and I won't compromise. So I'm wondering... what's planned for my character?"

The director cleared her throat, then answered her potential client. "We want this girl to be a teen idol—someone teens will watch and look up to. I don't *think* you'll have to violate anything you've just shared with me."

Whew! Charity walked out of the office on air. *I was honest about my convictions,* she thought. *If they'll give me a role like this and not ask me to compromise my values, maybe it's from God!*

She flashed back to the earlier reading she'd done with the director. Even though her script had some words she was uncomfortable using, she had ad libbed substitutions. And every time she'd seen God's name used as a swear word, she had changed it to something else. The director hadn't said anything. *Maybe, just maybe, this really is it,* she thought.

Charity and her parents began praying for God's direction. "I'm fortunate to have a really solid family," she said. "We pray about everything. Mom and Dad weren't totally sold on the idea, but neither did they want to stand in the way of something if it was from God. *That's* what we had to discern."

Charity left for Hawaii and continued to pray about her new-found opportunity. *Lord, keep me true to what YOU want for my life,* she prayed. *If this is something that would cause me to stray, I don't want it. Take it from me.*

As soon as Charity returned from her Easter vacation, the casting director was on the phone. "I have the producers on the other line. They loved your taped audition and are thrilled about you.

"I've discussed with them all the issues you're concerned about, Charity. They've made some changes in your character and have actually started writing scripts for her. Now you have to choose. They're coming here in two days to finalize things with you."

"What *kind* of changes?" Charity asked.

"Well," the director began. "This character will go through some adolescent issues that *all* teens struggle with."

"Like what?" Charity pressed.

"Your character is going to have an affair with an older, married man. After *that* affair, she'll fall in love with the lead singer of a rock band. They'll become sexually involved, and she'll eventually get pregnant."

Charity's mouth dropped open. "Adolescent issues that *all* teens struggle with?" she asked. "How many teens do *you* know who have affairs with married men? *I* don't know *any!* And I'm not going to portray one, either."

"Do you need some time to think about it?"

"I don't need *any* time to think!" Charity said. "I know exactly what my answer is. There is no way I can *ever* be a part of that. I'll never allow myself to represent those things; that's betraying everything I believe in. I couldn't live with myself."

The battle began. Producers pleaded with Charity to learn the distinction between *acting* and *reality.* Her school principal and music teacher also stressed that this would not have to affect her personal life—it was merely representing a fictional character. After all, isn't that what acting's all about?

Not in Charity's mind. "I want God's absolute best for my life," she says. "And I won't be happy outside of his perfect will for me. If he calls me to Africa and no one sees me again, that's OK. As long as I'm in the center of his will, I'll be fulfilled."

When I asked her what was happening now, Charity responded. "My principal isn't using me to escort visitors around the school anymore," Charity says with a laugh. "For a short while, I was sort of the 'chosen spokesperson.' The administrators were parading me in front of the school board and bragging about how I was going to bring fame to the school through 'Another World.'"

And the girl who took her place? "I was in the grocery store a couple of months ago," Charity recalls, "and saw her face on the cover of several magazines. In fact, *all* the soap mags had something on her.

"She's really cute. They had photos of her and the male co-star, who's a BABE! And I'm standing in line going *ooooh*. I have to admit: I battled with a little jealousy for a few seconds.

"I mean, that could've been *me!*" Charity says. "My dream of singing and acting was staring at me in full color. Suddenly it wasn't just words from producers; here she was in 3-D! And, yes, she's become a star—complete with riches, fame… *and the guy!*"

Standing in line, Charity began asking God why that couldn't have been her. Once she bought the magazine and read it, though, everything became clear.

"This new actress talked about how she prepared for her role. She said listening to extremely sexy music provided good motivation when memorizing her hot and steamy love scenes.

"And then I knew," Charity says. "There was *nothing* right about that. Everyone kept saying how acting and reality were two different things. But look at *her*—she's having to be influenced by the lifestyle in order to portray that kind of character. I could never do that.

"I don't live a glitzy life," Charity points out. "But I *do* live a life that's pleasing to God."

COMPROMISE OR PURITY?

It would have been easy for Charity to take the fame and the money, wouldn't it? She could have easily rationalized (like her teachers and principal *wanted* her to) that she could still live a pure lifestyle and only *act* the part of being sexually involved with someone.

But Charity knows that sexual purity is much more than an act. She knows that sexual purity involves her entire life.

Now, let me toss the question in *your* lap, OK? What specifically do *you* think is involved in sexual purity? What do you have to do in your own life to make certain that you are truly sexually pure?

In the next chapter, you'll have a chance to look at a variety of dating situations and decide if they qualify as coming under the heading of "sexually pure" or not.

Chapter Fifteen
WHAT DO YOU VALUE?

If you're like most teens I've met, you're probably wrestling with how far to go physically. And that's a great concern. After all, just how far CAN you go and still be sexually pure? I want to know what YOU think. Read through the following scenarios and answer the questions.

KYLE AND LORI

Kyle and Lori have been dating for three months. Lori goes to church regularly, but Kyle doesn't. She's signed a "True Love Waits" pledge card and plans to save herself for marriage.

When Kyle first asked her out, she was honest about her convictions, and he said he respected her beliefs. Once in a while he comes to church with her, but not consistently. Lori was ecstatic when Kyle first asked her out, and now that they've been together a while, she thinks she's falling in love with him.

Every now and then, things will get a little heated when they're saying good-bye. Her feelings go deep for Kyle, and it's really hard to stop kissing at the end of an evening.

After Friday night's football game, they went to the local pizza hangout before Kyle took her home so she could make the midnight curfew her parents had given them. To her surprise, though, the house was empty.

She invited him in to listen to some new CDs she'd only had for a week. They relaxed on the couch and began kissing. Before she knew it, Kyle's hand was underneath her blouse. Several thoughts raced through her mind. Even though she was flooded with wonderful physical feelings she'd never experienced before, she knew they'd crossed a boundary.

Here are some questions for you concerning this situation. Answer them honestly to yourself.

- ☛ Is Lori being sexually pure at this moment?
- ☛ What should she do right now?
- ☛ Should she continue to date Kyle?
- ☛ What can she do to make sure this doesn't happen again?

Something to think about: The problem here started long before Lori invited Kyle into her home that evening. In fact, it started long before their date that night.

Lori actually let down her guard as *soon as she started dating someone who wasn't a Christian.* Even though he attended church with her occasionally, it's obvious they don't share the same beliefs and values.

Her guard was let down even further when she invited Kyle into her house knowing they would be alone. When they became involved in prolonged kissing, Lori should have known they were headed for trouble.

If she doesn't act *quickly* and *decisively,* it probably won't be too long before she breaks her commitment to remaining sexually pure.

At this point, Kyle may begin pressuring her to give in. "There's nothing wrong with a little exploring," he may say. But if Lori is serious about her pledge to remain sexually pure, she won't allow herself to cross this boundary again.

DEREK AND DAWN

Derek's a high school senior and Dawn is in the eighth grade. She's had a crush on him forever, so you can imagine her delight when he finally asked her out for Saturday evening.

"We'll go to dinner," he said, "and then see what happens."

Her parents were concerned that she wanted to date such an older guy. Even though they shared her excitement about being asked out, they didn't give her permission to go.

But Dawn couldn't get Derek out of her mind, and she couldn't bring herself to turn him down. She lied to her parents and announced that she was spending the night at Debbie's house.

Derek picked her up there, and the two headed toward his favorite restaurant. After dinner, he suggested they drive to the lake so they could view the city lights reflecting off the water.

Dawn was flattered to have Derek give her such special treatment. It felt nice to have her doors opened and her meal paid for. When they got to the lake, however, he pulled her close and began kissing her passionately.

She was surprised at the sudden rush of feelings that engulfed her. She drew back and explained that she wasn't comfortable kissing on the first date.

"You're kidding!" Derek snapped. "I thought you were more mature than most girls your age. You sure *look* like it. But you're just a kid!"

He was getting angry, and Dawn didn't want to risk losing him. "I *am* mature, Derek!" she said as she scooted back into his arms.

Before she realized what was happening, Derek was on top of her. Even though they both kept their clothes on, Dawn felt as though she was nude.

What Does God Say about Premarital Sex?

Dear Susie:

I've been seeing this guy for a week and a half, and I really want to have sex with him, but I'm not sure how much of a sin sex is. I'm currently a virgin.

I've been brought up as a Christian, but I seem to be slipping away from my faith. It seems too hard to live by. I don't see sex as such a bad sin—it's not even listed in the Ten Commandments.

I'm not in love with my boyfriend, but I do like him. Please tell me what God says about premarital sex.

London, England

How much of a sin is premarital sex? Sin is sin. It's not like you can sin part way or something. You can't be a "little bit" pregnant. You're either pregnant, or you're not. You can't "sort of" murder someone. You either kill him, or you don't.

And yes, the Ten Commandments *do* talk about sex! God wouldn't have included adultery in the "Thou Shalt Nots" if it weren't a big deal.

God isn't a kill-joy. He's not sitting on his throne trying to come up with new ways to make your life miserable. He created sex as an incredibly wonderful gift. And when unwrapped at just the right time—on your wedding night—it serves as the ultimate in intimate bonding between you and your mate.

After reading this story, answer the following questions:

☞ Are Dawn and Derek being sexually pure?
☞ Why do you think Derek wanted to go out with Dawn?

Unwrapped too early, though, it becomes used and cheapened, and it creates jealousy, bitterness, and diseases.

You say you've been seeing a guy for a week and a half and want to have sex with him. A week and a half is hardly enough time to really get to know a person. Are you sure it's *sex* you're really wanting? Or could it be that you're very attracted to this guy (which is normal), and you want affection (because it feels good, and that's also normal), and you want to express to him that you care about him (which is also normal). And you *assume* that means you want to have sex with him.

I'm not convinced that's what you really want. I think you have a deep desire to be loved and affirmed. This guy in a week and a half has made you feel special and wanted, and you're interpreting those feelings as a foundation that's strong enough to handle the eternal bonding factor of sex.

You say you feel that you're slipping away from your faith. How 'bout taking all these feelings to the Lord? Be extremely honest with him. Tell him how far away you feel from him. Explain what you feel for this guy. Thank God for creating sex as a special gift. Ask him to help you see it through his eyes instead of the world's.

Then spend some time reading your Bible. Get involved in a Bible study. It's my guess after a few weeks of this, you won't feel far away from God any more. And as you grow closer to him, consider making a pledge to keeping your virginity until marriage. There's not a better gift you can present to your future husband than yourself... *all* of yourself.

☞ Why were Dawn's parents uneasy about their daughter being with an older guy?

☞ What specific guidelines should Dawn establish before dating any other guys?

Something to think about: Even though you may not understand why your parents won't allow you to date specific people, trust them. God doesn't expect you to always agree with and understand your parents, but he *does* command you to honor, obey, and respect them. If they won't let you go out with someone, *never* go behind their backs.

Dawn's parents didn't want her to date Derek for a good reason. Generally speaking, older guys are more experienced daters. They've been around. The reason they want to take out younger girls is often because they know a younger girl will look up to them and admire them. Therefore, chances are the guy will be able to do more physically with a younger girl. In other words, many times an older guy goes out with a younger girl with *this* on his mind: *This'll be a piece of cake. She's so flattered that I'm even paying attention to her, I'll be able to get anything I want!*

The fact that Derek had no concrete plans for the evening should have been a major warning sign for Dawn. *Always* have a set agenda when you're going out. Never assume anything. A guy who doesn't care enough to plan out the evening for you is a guy who's pretty selfish.

When Derek announced that he wanted to take Dawn to the lake, *she* should have suggested an alternate plan. When two people are parked in an isolated place, they're only looking for trouble.

After hearing Derek call her a "kid," Dawn should have said, "Yeah, I guess I am. And if *you're* the example of maturity, I guess I'll *never* be there! Take me home."

SETTING BOUNDARIES

Neither couple in these two stories had sex, but neither couple can honestly say they were living a sexually pure lifestyle, either. Remember, purity isn't an *act*, it's a *lifestyle*, a way of thinking for you as a young Christian woman.

Let me say it again: Sexual purity isn't simply keeping your virginity. *Anyone* can avoid intercourse. Purity means refusing to even "play around" with things that keep you from becoming all that God wants you to be.

In the case of the two couples in this chapter, they were "playing around" with their physical desires by allowing themselves to get into situations that could lead to trouble. Again, prolonged, deep kissing leads to petting and caressing... and this leads to intercourse.

So what is the best strategy for establishing and keeping sexual purity? How do you keep from getting in situations like the ones we've talked about in this chapter? The first thing you need to do is establish some physical boundaries and determine NOT to cross them! Also, determine that you will never date anybody who tries to get you to cross them.

I suggest you sit down and write out what you feel is permissible within a dating relationship. Pray about what you've expressed and talk to a Christian adult about it (like your parents, youth leader, or pastor). Here's another suggestion: Be specific when you set your boundaries. Don't think you can set them for yourself *while* you're out with a guy.

When I'm asked about setting boundaries, I usually offer this advice: Instead of trying to see how much you can get away with, ask yourself instead, "What would Jesus do?"

IT'S LIKE THIS

I believe that as a Christian teen who wants to establish godly dating relationships, you really want God's best for your life.

Make it your goal to grow as close to Jesus Christ as you possibly can. It works like this:

This circle represents Christianity. If you're a Christian, you're somewhere inside this circle. The dot in the middle represents Jesus Christ. YOU choose how close to the dot you're going to live your life.

There may be some things you can do when you're hanging out around the edge of the circle, but the closer you move to the dot in the middle, the more you realize the need to let go of the things you're clinging to on the outer edges.

How close do you want to live to Jesus Christ? He has an incredible plan for your life! He dreams B-I-G dreams for you. But those dreams will only become reality as you move closer to him.

Don't just ask yourself, "How much can I get away with and still be inside the circle? How much can I do and still be considered a Christian?" Ask yourself instead, "What more can I commit to God in order to grow closer to him? Is there anything else I can let go of to draw me nearer to his plan for my life?"

As you begin to establish dating relationships, let these questions guard your thinking. Instead of, "How far can I go and still be technically a virgin?" ask yourself, "What are the best ways to guard my purity? What specific fences can I build to ensure that I won't let down my guard?"

WHAT DO YOU CHERISH?

Try to think of your sexual purity as a valuable treasure, something that you will cherish until the day you are married.

If I gave you a couple of quarters to put in your purse, you probably wouldn't think much of it. If I gave you a silver dollar to keep in your purse, you'd probably try to remember not to leave it lying around in an open area. If I gave you a hundred dollars, you'd probably keep your purse with you. But if I placed a million dollars inside your purse, you'd guard it with your life... or you'd put it in a vault for safe keeping.

Your sexuality is just such a treasure. The question is, how much do you value it? The answer is found in how well you guard it. It is a priceless gift from God. Don't leave it up for grabs. Protect and hide it. That's what sexual purity is all about.

Mail Bag IV
QUESTIONS AND ANSWERS ABOUT GUYS!

Dear Susie:

There's a guy at school who likes me. He's really nice and sweet, but he's of a different race. This makes no difference to me, but my parents don't agree with interracial relationships.

Should I try to change my parents minds? Should I forget about him?

Saginaw, MI

Since God commands that we obey our parents, you have no choice but to refrain from dating him. Continue to be his friend. Talk to him at school, smile, and don't simply start snubbing him. But the truth is, you can actually be a good friend with a guy without developing an intimate relationship with him.

Ask your folks if the three of you can sit down and talk about it. (And don't yell. Talk in a normal, calm voice.) Remind them that you understand their feeling on interracial dating, but ask their permission for doing some "friendship" things. For instance, would they mind if you did things in large groups of people? Softball games, going to the mall, swimming? If they still disagree with you spending time with him, you'll need to sit down with him and explain that you value his friendship but you want to honor your parents.

Dear Susie:

My mom says she won't let me date at all. I think she's afraid I might have sex. But how can I do something if I don't even know what it is? I'm home-chooled and not exposed to lots of things. I don't even know what having sex really means.

Boca Raton, FL

I suggest you hop back to chapter two and ask your mom some of the suggestion questions I've listed. If you haven't pledged to remain sexually pure until marriage, let me encourage you to do so.

Share your commitment with your mom and ask her to support you in this pledge. She probably hasn't talked a lot about sex with you because she's uncomfortable with the subject. That's OK. Try to make it as easy on her as possible.

Remind her of your desire to be all God wants you to be, but also let her know you have some questions about sex. Explain that since you trust her wisdom, you'd rather hear about it from her than anyone else. Ask if the two of you can visit the library and look for some books that will provide the information you need.

Dear Susie:

There's this guy at my school, and he's been touching me and two of my friends in places we don't want him to touch.

Our principal found out and suspended him for three days. But I'm still scared he'll do it again. What should we do? How can we prepare?

Longview, TX

Your principal was right to suspend him, but I hope he also spoke with the boy's parents. This is wrong—in fact it's punishable by law! I understand your fear. No one likes to wonder if they'll be invaded or forced upon.

Avoid him if you can. If that's not always possible, then try not to be alone. Always have another friend with you when you walk through the halls, sit in the cafeteria, or go to the library.

It's my guess that since he's been suspended, he'll think twice before attempting to touch you again. But if it *does* happen again, go straight to the principal. The boy will probably be kicked out of school—which is exactly what needs to happen if he can't control his hands.

Dear Susie:

I had been going out with this guy for three months and eight days. A couple of days ago, he broke up with me because he said he doesn't need or want a girlfriend right now.

We were in love! I STILL love him! I'm hurting, but I try not to let it get the best of me. I don't want any other guy, because I KNOW he's the one. What should I do?

Campbellhall, NY

There's no way around it—breakups *hurt*. And the only thing that really heals the wound? Time. You've probably already heard things like, "there are more fish in the sea," and "he doesn't know what he gave up." But the truth is, if he broke up with you and says he doesn't need a relationship right now, there's really nothing you can do but accept that.

And that's tough. It's easier to tell you what *not* to do. DON'T try to get him back. That will only drive him further away and make him more determined that he made the right decision. Smile, be friendly, and don't hide from him. But don't go out of your way to see him, either.

Are there some other activities you can throw yourself into

right now? That will help take your mind off him and off the pain you're feeling from being apart. Strive to fill the void with something else. Deepen your other friendships, get more involved in your youth group, start a Bible study, or try out for the school play.

I know it doesn't feel like it, but I promise things will eventually get better.

Dear Susie:

How do you know if a guy likes you? I was at a school dance, and when I danced with this guy, he smiled and looked into my eyes. Does this mean he likes me? He looks at me a lot during class, too.

Then there's this other guy who goes to my church and my school. Whenever he sits behind me, he hits my hair or tosses something at me. Does this mean anything?

Alpine, TX

You've asked a very popular question. Many times it's hard to tell if a guy likes you. But we'll get to that in a second. Let's start with the beginning of your letter.

Saying that he smiled and looked into your eyes while dancing doesn't tell me much. He's supposed to look in your eyes while dancing. Where else could he look? Did he ask you to dance, or did you ask him? If he asked you, AND he's looking at you during class, chances are he likes you. It's obvious he's certainly *thinking* about you!

Now about the other guy who's hitting your hair.... Many times younger guys don't know how to get a girl's attention. They aren't as verbally skilled as some of the older guys, and they haven't been around girls enough to be comfortable with them. So they resort to doing things that bug us to get our attention. Unfortunately, many times this means punching us in the arm, tapping our shoulder then looking away, or hitting our hair.

I think he wants attention from you. If you'll start talking to him *before* he has a chance to hit your hair, I bet he'll soon stop.

Dear Susie:

A while back I broke up with my boyfriend because we didn't talk much. I really hurt his feelings and he wants to go out with me again.

I think I still like him, but I'm so confused. He's all I ever think about. I'd kind of like to go out with him again, but is it right?

Ontario, Canada

Is it right, meaning "is this a *moral* thing?" Or is it right, meaning "is this smart thing to do?" Unless you two were involved in something sinful, no, it's not an issue of something being morally right or wrong.

Is it the smart thing to do? I don't think so. You broke up because he wasn't a good communicator. Chances are he hasn't greatly improved those skills in the short time you've been apart. You probably miss him because you miss being in a relationship. It feels good to have somebody. It makes us feel connected and like we belong. Those are natural feelings, but they're *not* good reasons for getting together with someone. That's simply dating to be dating.

If you *do* get back together, you'll soon face the same frustration that led you to break up with him in the first place.

Get involved in some other activities so you can get your mind off of him. Continue to be nice to him, but don't make the mistake of getting back into a relationship that wasn't working in the first place.

Dear Susie:

I'm seventeen years old, and I've never had a boyfriend. What's wrong with me? All my friends have dated, and I constantly feel like I'm on the outside looking in. Every now and then I'm kind of moody, but generally speaking, I'm a lot of fun. Any advice?

George Lake, FL

Even though our society makes it look like being involved in an opposite-sex relationship is the most important thing in the world, it's not. Your relationship with Jesus Christ is what's ultimately important.

There's absolutely nothing in the world wrong with you. Many girls don't date at all until they get to college—then they date their heads off. And many don't date much in college but date a lot when they're out of college and starting their careers.

Your fulfillment and security can not come from a relationship with a guy. A guy can *enhance* your happiness, but he can't bring it. Only God can truly fill you with purpose and make you whole and secure. If you base all that on a relationship with a guy, and he dies or you break up, all your security and fulfillment is gone.

Too many people enter marriage looking for wholeness in the other person. The result? You have two halves that never make a whole. But two single people who have allowed God to make them whole will enter marriage whole and will have a loving, lifetime relationship.

So, what I'm saying is, know that you're normal. Believe that you're terrific. Trust that God has incredible plans for you (see Ephesians 3:20 for proof). Take advantage of the fact that you're *not* tied down right now and get involved in as many things as you can.

That's what I'm doing. I'm still single, and I'm taking advantage of it. Someday, when I'm married, I probably won't be able to do all the things I'm doing right now.

For instance, in four days I'm going to Thailand. Last year I spent a week and a half in Africa. I travel about every other weekend *within* the United States speaking to youth groups. I wrote eight books last year.

I wouldn't have gotten to do all that if I were married. So instead of thinking, *When am I going to get married?*, I'm enjoying life with as much gusto as I can. You do the same, and trust the Lord to bring just the right guy into your life at just the right time.

In chapter nineteen of this book, you will meet some people who are living exciting lives though single.

Dear Susie:

I was raped yesterday. I haven't told anybody, but I suspect some people know. You see, this guy was sexually harassing me and he got in trouble for it. He's been looking for revenge ever since. Should I tell someone or just drop it unless he comes around again? I really don't want anybody to know!

Humberside, England

I wish I were with you right now. I'd give you a big hug and tell you how very very sorry I am that you've experienced such a nightmare! What happened to you was a crime and a sin on the part of the perpetrator.

I want you to know that when God looks at you, he sees a pure and whole young lady. This is NOT your fault. Please don't berate yourself with false guilt. Satan would love to confuse and frighten you with that right now. Continue to look to your heavenly Father for strength and courage.

Please, please tell your parents and ask them to go *with* you to the authorities. Everything in the world must be done to make sure this guy NEVER approaches you again.

I know you don't want this secret out, but your parents really need to know. This is way too big for you to try to handle by yourself. You can't. And you can't keep it inside, either. Eventually, it *will* come out. It might take a few months or a few years, but it will come out in the form of anger or depression.

After you talk with your parents, ask them to help you find a Christian counselor who can walk you through the grief and healing process.

PART 5

Creating Positive Dating Memories

How can a person's attitude affect others?

"During my first two years of high school, I lived in a really small town. I had a LOT of trouble fitting in simply because I didn't like it. I had a rotten attitude. Because of that, people started sensing I didn't want to be there, and it became very hard to make friends. A good or bad attitude can make a WORLD of difference to those around you. "

Neal Coomer, East to West

Are guys as concerned about their appearance as girls are about THEIRS?

"We want to look good, but most of us aren't *obsessed* with it. Seems like girls spend a lot of time in front of the mirror—every hair has to be in just the right place. If I'm having a 'bad hair day,' it doesn't wreck my perspective or anything."

Matt Gowler, 12

Chapter Sixteen
HOW DO I KNOW IF I'VE FOUND THE RIGHT ONE?

...when looks aren't everything...

You adore his dimples and have memorized the way his lips curl when he smiles. You like everything about the way he looks. But how do you know if the guy you like is really right for you?

Let's admit it: We're all attracted to a handsome face, especially one that is recently splashed with great-smelling cologne. But beyond his good looks, what else should we be considering when looking for the right guy to date?

We've all known girls who dated guys they fell head over heels in love with... only to be disappointed later. Obviously, there are more important things than a face and a body.

How, when you're "falling in love" with a guy, can you know

if he could be the right one? Here are five questions to ask yourself before you fall head over heels for the wrong guy.

1. What are his values? No one wants to date a clone, and many times opposites are attracted to each other. But fun differences in *personality* are one thing, conflicting *beliefs and values* are another.

When it comes to basic values, what does this guy believe? Are you pro-life, but he's pro-choice? That's a big difference. Are you high on church involvement, but he's shying away from even approaching the church *building?* Again, big diff.

How deeply does he value sexual purity, if at all? What about movies and music? Do you share the same beliefs concerning how the media influence us?

Having shared values is one of the strongest ways to maintain a close bond with someone you care about. If your guy's values clash with yours, that could mean trouble, either now or down the road.

2. How does he treat his mother? Any guy can make a good impression when he's *trying* to, but what about the times he doesn't have to? Often the true self will emerge when he's with his family. And if a guy treats his mom with respect, chances are he'll do the same with his dating partners.

See if this scenario looks familiar:

Mr. and Mrs. Brown had asked Jarrod to invite Jennifer over for dinner. "Instead of always going out," his mom said, "bring her over here a few times. We'd enjoy getting to know her better."

Jennifer arrived right on time, and Jarrod greeted her at the door. Mrs. Brown appeared from the kitchen to greet her, then continued some last-minute preparations for dinner.

Jarrod flopped down on the sofa and clicked on the TV. Mrs. Brown, her arms loaded with dishes, had to walk to and from the dining room to get everything in place.

The phone rang a few minutes later, and after the fourth ring, Jarrod yelled, "Mom, can you get that? I'm trying to watch something!"

Do you see anything wrong with this picture? If you were in Jennifer's shoes, what would Jarrod's behavior tell you? Is he a gentleman? Does he offer to help around the house? Does he open doors for his mom and treat her like a lady? When he talks to his mom, is there a gentleness there? Or does he brush her off, seem embarrassed by her, or even appear put out by her?

How a guy treats people in general is important, but how he treats his mother could give you a clue what you're in for if you get serious with the guy.

3. How does he handle responsibility? Nobody enjoys being in a relationship with an irresponsible person, and you should make sure the guy you date shows a strong sense of responsibility before you commit yourself to him on any level.

Let's take a look at a young woman whose boyfriend isn't all he could be in this area:

Joel often tells Stacie that he'll drop by at 7 P.M. so they can study together. But it's usually 7:30 before he actually shows up. In fact, Joel seems to be consistently late every time they get together.

Everybody knows Joel is very good in wood shop, and about three weeks ago, the drama teacher asked him if he would build one of the props for the all-school play. Joel agreed to do it, but hasn't been to any of the prop meetings. When Stacie asked him about it, he admitted he hadn't even started the prop and would probably get around to telling the drama teacher that he really has no time to do it.

Do you see some warning signs for Stacie? More importantly, do you see any of Joel in the guy *you* like? If you're wanting someone who'll remain solid, take an especially close look at some of the following questions.

Does he show up late a lot of the time? Part of responsibility is being on time. I'm not talking about running a little late once in a while—that happens to everyone. But does he *consistently* mess up his own schedule and, therefore, arrive late for *you?*

Does he do what he says he will? Does he finish the projects he starts? Does he always look for the easy way out of situations? Does he get bored quickly and move on to something else?

These things will eventually affect his relationship with you.

4. What are others saying about him?

What other people think about a guy you like is important, and you should pay attention to what you hear. I'm not asking you to take a poll about him, and gossip is *always* wrong. But if trusted adults are all saying negative things about him—or are even asking some serious questions—that ought to raise some red flags.

Think about it: Teachers, your youth leader, and coaches are usually very dependable. Do they have major concerns about the character of the guy you like? If they do, instead of getting defensive and trying to argue with them, ask if you can make an appointment to sit down with them and hear what they have to say.

5. Where does he stand with Jesus Christ?

I've saved the most important question for the last. That question is this: Does your friend have a relationship with Jesus Christ? For that matter, does he even claim to be a Christian? And if he does, do his actions match his words? Can you *see* the evidence of a relationship with Jesus in his life?

If a guy wants to date you, you need to make sure that he shares the same relationship with God that you have. If he doesn't share that faith, you shouldn't even *think* about going out with him, let alone being emotionally attached to him.

Here's a story of a young lady who had a decision to make:

For almost four months, Ashley boasted about having a major crush on Brent. So she was ecstatic when he finally started paying attention to her.

"You wanna go on a picnic Sunday morning?" he finally asked. "I know this great place."

"I go to church on Sundays, Brent," Ashley said.

"Well, can't you skip once?"

Ashley could have skipped church and gone with Brent, or she could stick to her convictions and go to church as she always had. Or she could have suggested that Brent come with her to church, *then* go with him on the picnic.

But the real issue here isn't whether Brent would have gone to church with Ashley. You can talk just about any guy who likes you into simply attending church with you. What matters most is where he *really* stands with Jesus Christ. If the guy you like doesn't know God, then what you *should* be discussing as your deepest form of commonality isn't even a part of his most casual conversation.

If you're striving to be all God wants you to be, you'll be fighting an uphill battle by dating a nonbeliever or someone who isn't as serious about his faith as you are. Don't compromise. Wait for a guy who has a *real* relationship with Jesus!

IN CONCLUSION...

So, you think you might have found the guy for you? You like everything about him—even his goofy laugh! Right now, you're having fun just getting to know him. It may seem like there couldn't possibly be anything wrong with this relationship.

But before you allow yourself to become too emotionally attached, step back, take a look at this guy, and honestly ask yourself the questions I've listed here. Ask God for wisdom to see things in your friend that you might not want to look at.

Don't compromise on these things, either. Make sure that this guy has the right stuff to move into a dating relationship. Don't commit yourself until you know for sure if he really is the kind of guy you want to be with.

God loves you, and he doesn't want you to settle for anything less than the best.

Chapter Seventeen
SECRETS TO
SUCCESSFUL
RELATIONSHIPS

For great friendships, look inside your heart.

Jamie and Eric dated for a year and a half during college, and they were the envy of the entire campus. They just seemed to have it together in their relationship. They weren't perfect, and they had misunderstandings, but they always worked through them. And today? They have a successful marriage.

Hellllooo... here's what you've been waiting to hear!

Kathi and Tyson went to the same university that Jamie and Eric attended. All four were friends and often double-dated. But Kathi and Tyson's relationship was always rocky. They fought frequently and had a hard time working through the difficulties. They were married after graduation, but the marriage didn't last long. They were divorced after two years.

Cyndi and Mark started dating in high school. Though they

enjoyed each other's company, he broke up with her after three months. Cyndi then dated Brian, but she broke up with *him* after a month. Next she dated Andy, Mike, Thad, and Craig, and whether they broke up with her or she broke up with them, she simply wasn't good at establishing and maintaining solid relationships.

You may know some people who fall into the above categories. They either have great relationships or they don't. Though break-ups are normal and mostly unavoidable, there *are* a few things you can do to build healthy relationships with the opposite sex.

Since most connections begin in the *heart,* let's use the word *HEART* (H.E.A.R.T.) to discuss the secrets that are found in great relationships.

THE H.E.A.R.T. OF THE MATTER

H o **Hear the other person.** Successful relationships are built on a foundation of good communication skills. A skilled conversationalist knows how to listen well. We like to feel that our friends are genuinely interested in what we're feeling. Of course, that includes the people we date.

When you're in a relationship with a guy, remember that he wants you to *hear* what he has to say. Nobody, guys included, likes to be around people who have to be talking all the time.

If your guy friend is not an open person, or if he seems to have trouble starting conversations, just ask questions that will draw him out. Seek to discover his opinions, his strengths, and his hobbies. Often, we're so worried about running out of things to say that we overcompensate by talking too much. Instead of doing that, just ask questions to get the other person talking.

If you learn good communication skills and don't monopolize the conversation, you will establish great relationships and more than likely will keep a friendship, even if the dating relationship ends.

E o **Enjoy common interests.** One of the secrets of terrific relationships is having a variety of things you enjoy doing together. Often, discovering what those common interests are is half the fun!

Exploring what you have in common takes time and energy— but the rewards are worth the effort! One reason many dating relationships don't last long is that one person gets bored with the other. Doing things together that you both enjoy will not only prevent boredom, it will build a fun relationship at the same time.

Don't sit back in a relationship and let the guy make all the decisions. Give *your* input on what you'd like to do when you're together. Maybe you'd like to go horseback riding. Tell him! Maybe he wouldn't suggest that because he doesn't know you enjoy horses. He plays baseball? How do you know if you'd enjoy baseball if you've never tried? Go to a batting cage together and let him teach you how to hit.

Take sailing lessons. Bake cookies together, then deliver them to your friends. Ride bikes (ever thought of renting a bicycle built for two?). There are literally hundreds of things you can enjoy together!

A o **Allow each other space.** Relationships often crumble because one of the people involved felt smothered. Teen girls often cling too tightly to their dating partner for fear of losing him. Don't give in to that temptation. Remember, the people everyone wants to be with are those who have the ability to care without possessing.

Think about the best marriage you've ever seen. Both partners give each other the space they need to feel whole as individuals. One partner isn't threatened when the other is away, involved in activities with other friends.

The guy you like needs to know that your life is fulfilled whether he's a part of it or not. It's nice that he *enhances* your life, but he can't be the reason for your security or happiness. When he becomes *that* important to you, he'll start feeling cornered.

Terrific relationships are the product of two people who enjoy each other's company but maintain other friendships as well. If your boyfriend says he can't go out Friday night because he wants to be with the guys, give him that space. He *needs* time with other male friends. That's healthy.

There are times *you* need to simply hang out with your girlfriends. But if the guy you're dating seems to get progressively more and more possessive, he's probably insecure and afraid that he'll lose you. That's not a healthy relationship.

To avoid these problems, take the time to honestly discuss the need for *both* of you to spend time with your family and other friends. Try to do this at the very beginning of your dating relationship.

R o **Respect each other.** Every successful couple has a o large ingredient of respect in the center of their relationship, and the area where respect is needed most for teen couples is in physical and emotional intimacy.

We've already chatted about this earlier... but I want to emphasize it again: Don't wait until you're in a dating relationship to establish your physical boundaries! Create your strategy *now*.

I challenge you to sit down with your parents or your youth leader and discuss physical intimacy with them. Ask them to help you create some solid dating guidelines so you can establish healthy relationships *before* you begin dating someone.

(For more detailed information on a specific ladder of intimacy, check out *What Hollywood Won't Tell You About Sex, Love and Dating* by Greg Johnson and Susie Shellenberger, Regal Publishing.)

T o **Tote a trainable spirit.** To be successful at *any-* o *thing* in life, we need a teachable spirit. That includes our relationships. Someone who is trainable will go far in life because she's willing to learn new ways of doing things. On the other hand, someone who is so stubborn that she refuses to bend most likely won't have a fantastic relationship.

I produced several plays and musicals when I worked as a high school drama teacher. When I auditioned students for various roles, you might think I searched for the most talented people to play the lead parts. But you know what? I usually gave the biggest roles to students who were not as talented as some of the other teens who tried out.

When I cast Chelsey as the female lead in *Bye Bye Birdie* instead of Jill, people couldn't believe it. A few parents even called to express their concerns: "Are you sure? Chelsey's just not as talented as Jill."

But I had a secret. I knew that teachable students would be more willing to listen to my instructions and try different approaches as I guided them. These students were *far* more valuable to me than the more talented kids who already knew they could sing and act but were unwilling to be reshaped.

It works the very same way in relationships. If your date's parents have suggestions, listen. If they have doubts about a concert you already have tickets to, be flexible. Be willing to change plans if necessary. In other words, don't always demand your way.

Relationships that last are flexible. They have the ability to bend because the people involved refuse to be stubborn or demand "their rights." Instead, they are tender-hearted and teachable.

THE BOTTOM LINE

Break-ups are inevitable (unless you're getting married), and these secrets aren't guarantees that your dating relationships will last forever. But *every* successful relationship *does* have the elements I've listed.

Chances are if you live out the above ingredients, you'll still have a *friendship*, even after the *dating* aspect is over. That's because you've built your relationship on a solid foundation!

GUY TALK

What Makes Me Respect a Girl

"When I see a well-liked girl trying to include someone who isn't popular, it doubles my respect for her. This can mean talking with someone who's eating alone or simply reaching out to those around her.

"When I see a young lady refusing to participate in gossip, and determined not to make herself look better at someone else's expense, she *commands* my respect.

"The girls I respect are the ones who let *me* make the first contact! Someone who's always calling me or approaching me in the hall takes away the challenge.

"I find myself really attracted to a girl who's involved in her church, consistent in attendance, and growing spiritually."

—Denton, 17

"*Lifestyle* is where my respect is gained or lost. This includes attitude, reputation, values—even talk. For instance, when I hear a girl cussing in the hallway, my respect for her is immediately lost. It's not only offensive, but it takes away her femininity. That's a definite turn-off for me.

"On the other hand, when a girl has high standards and holds high expectations of *me,* I not only *respect* her but I want to be with her.

"I have no respect for girls who are casual with sex or try to tempt the guys they're with. That's just not attractive to me. I like a girl who shares my morals."

—Kevin, 16

"A girl who takes a strong stand morally *really* pumps my respect. I'm talking about a girl who will say, 'No, I won't watch that video (or movie or whatever) because God wouldn't be pleased.' Instead of jeopardizing her relationship with me, it just makes my respect for her soar!

"I also respect a girl with good social skills... someone who handles herself well in formal and informal situations. Someone who is well-mannered and disciplined makes others feel good about being around them. I can't help but respect a young lady like that.

"I *don't* respect a girl who simply follows the crowd. That takes away her individuality and also tells me she probably doesn't have much respect for herself. When a girl is simply *herself,* the uniqueness of her own personality is displayed—and that's worth respecting!"

—Mitch, 16

"The biggest respect factor for me is a girl's relationship with Christ. When I meet a young lady who's totally in love with God—and shows it outwardly—she immediately has my respect.

"I also watch how a girl relates to other guys. I appreciate a girl who is well-rounded in her relationships. Does she include other guys in her conversations or is she focused single-mindedly on me? I enjoy being friends with several people. Therefore, I respect a girl who does the same."

—Drew, 17

"I come from a very close-knit family, therefore, I respect a lady who maintains that same kind of relationship with her own family.

"My dad's a pastor, so church has always been a top priority in my life. When I see a young lady really getting involved in her church and taking responsibility (like teaching a Sunday school class or helping out in the nursery) it makes me respect her. This shows me she's at church because she *wants* to be, not simply because she thinks she *should* be."

—Eric Champion, contemporary Christian artist

Chapter Eighteen
DATES TO REMEMBER, DATES TO FORGET

What will you remember five years from now?

What makes a date memorable? Is it the cologne he's wearing, how he treats you, the warmth of the evening? Well, there are actually many *different* things that can make a date stand out forever in your mind.

Yikes! Get me out of here!

I asked a few adults to think back to their most memorable dates—good and bad—and what made them a special event or a nightmare. Maybe you'll get some ideas on what matters and what doesn't from what they share.

Let's start with the bad ones.

Bravo! Great date!

Where to, Lady?

"A date I'll never forget (but would *love* to) was with a guy who didn't even bother coming to the porch to get me. I had to meet him outside in the car. He wasn't any better by the end of the date, either. Instead of walking me to the door at the end of the evening, he just dropped me off at the curb."

—Jennifer

A formal fiasco

"I went to a formal dinner party with my date. It sounded fun, but it turned out to be a nightmare. She argued with me during the entire evening. She chose to drive (don't ask me why) and picked me up in this beat-up Chevette that couldn't go over 40 mph. The second I slid into the car... BOOM... she exploded like a volcano. She was a nice girl; it was just a weird night."

—Jim

Sight unseen

"My absolute worst date was a blind date. I agreed to go out with this guy without even knowing him. He picked me up on a motorcycle, he had tattoos all over his arms, and we had absolutely *nothing* in common. To make matters worse, my pants ripped during dinner and I had to wrap my sweater around my waist. If I learned *anything* from the evening, it was to know the person before going out."

—Shirley

In English this time?

"One of the worst dates I've ever had was in college. I had gone out a few times with a foreign guy. He invited me to spend some time with his family, so I accepted. They were from Kuwait, and *none* of them spoke English.

"I was trying to communicate and make the best of the situation, when all of a sudden his mom pulled out a pair of tweezers from her purse and started plucking my eyebrows!"

—Marsha

Gettin' picky

"My most horrible date was about five years ago. The UPS man kept trying to set me up with a friend of his. Finally—after several weeks of saying no—I reluctantly agreed to go out with him.

"When he rang my doorbell, I *almost* slammed the door and hid under the bed. He was old, fat, and bald. I gathered my courage and left with him. He *wanted* to take me to dinner and a movie. But *I* was determined to get through the evening as quickly as possible, so I agreed only to the movie part.

"About halfway through the movie (around 9:15 P.M.), I said, 'Tomorrow's Sunday and I have to teach a Sunday school class. I really should get home.' So we left the theater. My motto for all bad dates is, 'Always keep a toothpick in your mouth.' I quickly reached into my purse and started chewing on a toothpick so he wouldn't even *try* to kiss me good night. It worked."

—Brenda

Do I have another bid?

"The worst date *I've* ever had was with a guy I met at an auction. I was holding a lamp and he approached with the line, 'I'll give you $30 for that lamp if you'll have dinner with me.' I didn't even *know* him, but I agreed to go out... against my better judgment. He was a lawyer, so I remember thinking, *Well, at least he has a good job. Maybe it won't be that bad.*

"Big mistake. After all, he *could* have been an ax-murderer for all *I* knew. As I walked toward his car, I had a sinking feeling that this would be an evening I'd love to forget. His car was really messy. In fact, he had to clean off the seats and the floorboard just so I could sit down. It was really gross."

—Sherri

And for the lady?...

"My worst date was in the ninth grade. My best friend arranged for me to go to the school dance with a friend of a friend. Gary (my date) stood around leaning up against the gym wall with his sport coat open, feeling the lining vibrate from the loud music of the band.

"After the dance, we went to the town hangout for a Coke... or so I *thought*. It turned out that Gary only brought enough money for *one* Coke. He drank it and ordered *me* a glass of water!"

—Anna

As you can tell, it doesn't take much to turn a potentially fun evening into a disaster. But the exciting thing is that it also doesn't take much to turn an ordinary evening into a special night. You can make help build positive memories for the guys you date. As you read the following stories of great dates, you'll notice that it doesn't take a lot of money, new clothes, or an extravagant atmosphere to give your date a night you'll both cherish forever!

Happy birthday to me!

"My most memorable date was with a guy who really worked hard to make the entire evening special for me. He was in college and worked part time at a local television station. He began the date by taking me by the station and introducing me to everyone. I loved it! Even though it was a local thing, it was still fun to meet the news and weather personalities that I watched on TV every night.

"Then we went to a really fun and wild ice cream place. He had told the waiters ahead of time that it was my birthday, so when we arrived, they asked me to stand on top of the table while the whole staff sang 'Happy Birthday' to me.

"He took me home afterward, but before he left he gave me a book of poems along with seven other wrapped birthday gifts with instructions to open one every day during my birthday week. They were really fun gifts—some of them were just little ordinary things, but it was so special to have something to open each day.

"He *could* have just bought one nice gift, but he put so much thought and time into buying several smaller gifts and wrapping each one. By the end of the week, I felt like a queen!"

—Vicki

With these rings...

"One of my most memorable dates was actually a *double* date. My friend Chris and I decided we'd go to great lengths to plan a creative evening for two girls.

"We went to a store that had several gum ball machines and kept putting quarters in them until we both got two rings the same size. Then we had our pictures taken at one of those inexpensive photo booths at the mall. We then cut out our faces and glued them to the rings. It was really corny and funny!

"We picked up our dates and brought them back to my parents' house and made them shrimp cocktail. While they were munching on that, we grilled chicken and made some green beans. We served the meal with candlelight, then loaded up the car and went to the park.

"We opened the trunk and pulled out Welch's sparkling grape juice and plastic glasses. We sat near the fountain drinking juice and talking. Next, we presented them each with a rose and our crazy rings. They died laughing! We told them they had to wear the rings the rest of the evening. The whole date was a lot of fun!"

—Doug

The white zone is for...

"My best date was during college. Bobby was really creative. He treated me to a nice birthday dinner, then drove me to the airport. As we got out of the car, he opened his trunk, grabbed two suitcases, and handed *me* one. 'Act like it's really heavy,' he said.

"We went to a crowded section of the airport and sat down. He then opened his luggage and began pulling out all this birthday stuff... party favors, cake, etc. Then he told me to stand on top of a nearby chair. As I did, he began shouting: 'Ladies and gentlemen! This is Kay. Today is her nineteenth birthday. Please join us in celebrating, and help me sing *Happy Birthday*.'

"It was hilarious! I mean we didn't even *know* these people, and here we were having cake and punch with them. Afterward, an old lady edged next to Bobby, and said, 'Young man, I like your style!'"

—Kay

Impulsive flowers

"I've had some pretty creative dates. I have to admit, I was pretty romantic back in high school. Occasionally—when my girl was dropped off by the bus at her stop—I'd drive up with a bouquet of flowers. Today, I write a lot of poetry for my date, because it's part of who I am. And I still give flowers the on spur of the moment."

—Mark

A romantic day

"I'll never forget a date I had on Valentine's Day. It was an *event*. He picked me up around noon and took me to a house that was in the process of being built. The studs were up, but there wasn't any sheet rock. He spread a big blanket on the concrete and served me lunch. (He must have spent all morning in the kitchen.) He made pot roast, green beans, rolls, and iced tea.

"Afterward, he took me boating and we just talked for a long time. It was great! By this time it was close to evening, so he took me home and set up a table in the garage of my parent's house. He pulled out a big sign he had painted that read 'Happy Valentine's Day!' and placed it in the corner.

"Then he lit some candles and pulled out *another* dinner he had made ahead of time and had waiting at my house for me: chicken, carrots, and chocolate cheesecake with strawberries on top."

—Kathy

Come right home

"One of my best dates was a recent one with my wife. She called me at work and instructed me to come straight home. When I walked into the house, I was told to go directly into the bedroom. She had a pair of shorts and a T-shirt ready for me to change into, and told me to head out back as soon as I had changed.

"Our back yard is surrounded by a small neighborhood lake. When I walked outside, she had dinner fully prepared and waiting in a row boat. Definitely a fun memory."

—Paul

Campus life

"My best date was with a guy I started dating in high school. Tim fixed fettuccine ahead of time, packed his mom's china and table settings, picked me up, and drove me to the mall of a nearby college campus. He opened up the trunk and hauled out a table, tablecloth, rose, dishes—everything—and served me dinner.

"He had also arranged for a friend of his (who plays the French horn) to serenade us during the meal. Needless to say, I felt like a queen... and about a year later, I married him."

—Jana

After hours

"My wife and I dated over four years before we got married. So I was constantly trying to think of different and creative things to do when we went out. Sometimes we'd go to the mall after the stores were closed and just walk around or slide down the banister of the escalator after it had been turned off.

"One time I made her a picnic lunch and we ate it on the roof of a big high-rise. Another time I got permission to go to a golf course after it was closed, and we had a picnic on the greens."

—James

Toying with me

"Even though we broke up, I have some *great* memories of a guy I used to date. He was always bringing me fun, creative things. One time he brought me some clacking balls. They probably didn't cost over a dollar, but I loved them! They were just two little balls that made firecracker noises when you bumped them together.

"Another time he brought me this really neat water gun with a headband connected to it. It had a little tube that went from the band on your forehead to the gun, and when I pulled the trigger, water came out of a hole in the band on my forehead! It was hilarious.

"Then another time he gave me a humongous bubble-blower. I mean, this thing made ten-foot bubbles. I loved it! He was forever bringing me little things he'd get out of gum ball machines—miniature animals, super balls, rings."

—Lynda

Just plain fun

"Some of my best dates centered around just good, old-fashioned fun. One time we went to the state capital. Another time we stopped by the park and played Frisbee golf."

—Sylvia

A long, long drive

"One of my favorite dates was with a guy I went to a softball tournament with. We were in college, and after the games were over, he said, 'Let's drive to Amarillo for breakfast.' We both lived in Oklahoma City! It took us four and a half hours to get there, and another four and a half to get back. We ate breakfast and turned right around and came home. But it was really fun, because it gave us uninterrupted time to talk and really get to know each other."

—Nancy

An ordinary night

"One of my most fun dates was with another couple. We started out with dinner, then headed to my parents' house. We sang camp songs and just had a crazy time doing *ordinary* stuff. Around 9 P.M. we were hungry again, so we baked chocolate chip cookies, then went to play miniature golf to burn off the calories."

—Rhonda

Your play, mom

"My most memorable date was the first time I went out with the man whom I eventually married. We went to dinner then back to my place and played UNO with my mom. It was safe, comfortable, and fun. It was also important because it helped my mom to feel good about the relationship."

—Meredith

What are things guys do that probably make God laugh?

"Guys who make themselves out to be more than they really are have to make God laugh. So many guys are on an ego-power trip. The get carried away with their own knowledge and begin thinking they're on the same level with God, and that's just ridiculous"

Anson Dawkins, Dawkins and Dawkins

Do guys like to get notes from girls?

"Yes. Guys love to know someone is looking at them. I *lived* for notes from girls. Even if the girl who sent it wasn't cute, it was still fun to get a note from someone who was looking at *me!*"

Eric Dawkins, contemporary Christian artist

Chapter Nineteen
CELEBRITIES AND SINGLENESS

It's easy to think the *grass is greener on the other side of the fence*, especially when it comes to romance. Imagine this scene: It's spring, and couples all around you have been basking in the warm glow of love. Your response? *Lucky dogs. I'd be a whole lot happier if I could be involved in a great dating relationship too. So, how about it, Lord. Isn't it my turn yet?*

It's tempting to start thinking that you'll *never* find the right guy. And when *that* happens, your thoughts go wild, *What if... I never find the right person? What if I'm... single?*

Well, that's a real possibility. You *could* be single for a lifetime. But what makes the situation even harder to swallow is when you see married Christians in the spotlight who seem to have it all together. You know, the Steven Curtis Chapmans and the Michael W. Smiths who write songs about their spouses and speak openly about their children.

But what about the Christian celebrities who are single? How do they handle the solo step? What are they looking for in a mate (and are they even looking)? And when they go on dates, what kinds of stuff do they do?

Let me introduce you to six popular Christian artists who have a lot to say about the possibility of being single forever. It may surprise you how similar their views are to your own and those of many young Christians you know.

Before we get to our question-and-answer time, let's meet the cast:

Cindy Morgan: This powerhouse popster is often described as the Mariah Carey of Christian music. She grew up in Tennessee.

Pam Thum: She's a Native American with solid songwriting abilities and a silky voice to match.

Carman: He grew up on the mean streets of New York, often using his fists to survive. Through the years, his killer voice has touched thousands with the gospel.

Kirk Sullivan: This lead vocalist of 4HIM makes his home in Atlanta, Ga.

Mark Lowry: This Texas native is one of the funniest comedians in the business. But he also dishes out some serious stuff on singleness.

Ji Lim: Born in South Korea, Ji moved to the United States when he was six. He pursued a career in classical music, then plunged into Christian pop.

LET'S TALK...

Susie: *How do you handle your singleness?*
Cindy: I've come to realize that singles need to enjoy life the way it is. We need to be present-minded.

What do I mean? This: When I step on stage and sing, I focus on having a good time and enjoying the moment. But if I spend all my time thinking about my personal life and what isn't quite right, then I end up missing life. If I let my frustrations drag me down, then everything that could happen won't because I'm dwelling on unreality.

Cindy Morgan

I encourage guys and girls to examine where they are in life. Look around and notice the beautiful day. Go out and play football or volleyball. Fill your time with joy. Focus on a solution to your loneliness, not the problem. Glance at the problem and gaze at God. My pastor said this to me, "People gaze at the problem, but they only *glance* at God—who's the solution."

If we focus on what's good, then our lives will be happier.

Pam: I don't know if every woman is like me, but when I'm involved with someone, I tend to think, "What can I do to help them get their goals?"

I pour my life into my date. That's fine, but you also have to strike a balance. The key for me lies in maintaining time for my friends, because it's so easy to think you don't need anybody but him. It's also important to stay involved with church functions.

And during those times when I'm *not* dating anyone, I reach out. I see if there's someone I can visit at the nursing home once a week. It's a cool thing to do with the guy you're dating, too, because you can see how they respond in situations.

The bottom line: Think of things to keep your life full. Above all, our ultimate source should be God. That's certainly easy to say, but it takes a lot of work. None of us knows how much longer we have. Therefore, we have to give on a daily basis to everyone around us. They in turn give back, and it helps fulfill us so we don't need just that one person.

Kirk: I think I deal with it the way everybody deals with it. A while back Carman and I were on the Young Messiah Tour together. He and I were the only two single boys on the tour. We hung out together and began talking extensively about our singleness. I thought he would have some secret spiritual way he dealt with it. But, he deals with it the same way everyone else does: He keeps the matter in prayer, focuses on his walk with God but keeps his eyes open for a mate. And that's exactly what I do.

There are good days and bad days. There are days I wish I had someone here with me and there are days I'm glad I'm alone. One thing single people don't have is marriage problems. Once in a while I see that and I go, "Man, I'm glad I don't have that problem."

Ji: That's a deep question. But I've decided that I'm not grounding my life in "dating" relationships... or even a career or money. I'm grounding my life in God alone. That's how I'm handling my singleness.

It's a hard truth to live out because God's not physical. He's not there to hold you and hug you. Even though his word is there and the Holy Spirit is within us—it's still a struggle.

To get practical, music helps me a lot. I can release a lot of my frustrations or loneliness just by sitting down at the piano and playing. Friends and family help. But trusting that God knows what's best helps the most.

I also believe that if you're not content being single, you won't be content being married. If you're not where you should be as a person or in your walk with Christ, you're never going to find fulfillment in marriage. It's not an answer to life's problems. In fact, it's a testing ground, because you're bringing in a whole other person—a different dimension into your life and you're responsible for them.

I really believe God knows what he's doing and I trust in that. As for the loneliness, Jesus was lonely a lot of times, and how did he cope with it? He talked to his Father a lot. I do that a lot, too.

Susie: *When it comes to the whole dating-and-relating scene, what are some of the biggest mistakes guys and girls often make?*

Cindy: DON'T SETTLE. I think it's real important to have a grasp on who you are before you get married. Then figure out the kind of person you want to spend your life with.

When you're dating and wanting to be in a relationship there's nothing else that's more important to you. You're so focused on it you get obsessed with it. Many people think, *I've got to be married. There's just nothing more important to me.*

Suddenly, they're in dangerous territory. They end up looking for contentment in a feeling. That's a big mistake.

Pam: Don't tell someone you're in love with that "God told me that you are the one for me." All that's going to do is turn them off and put up bigger walls. If they're not responding, then you need to let go and take it to the feet of Jesus and say, "OK God, I thought I heard your voice. I'm confused." You cannot control another human being's will. They have choices. God hasn't made anyone a robot.

Look at the character of the Holy Spirit. He never pushes—he simply leads. If a relationship is of God then there will be peace for both parties. I know sometimes it's timing, but you still have to back off and let him make his decision. If you're obsessed with that person, you won't be open to something else God may have for you.

Carman: Some Christians make the mistake of thinking that God has revealed to them a person they were meant to marry—only, the other person doesn't agree.

If you think God has told you to marry someone, then that person will know, too. I've had some situations where people write me and say, "It's God's will for us to be married and have children." When God is in it, then both parties know.

Kirk: When you're in a dating relationship but find you're constantly asking God if this is the right one... then he or she probably isn't.

I think when the *right* person comes into your life, you won't even have to ask. That's something you'll know. And if you're walking right—reading the Bible and seeking God's will—then you're not going to miss it.

Mark: Know what? One is a whole number. Each time I get lonely, I remind myself of this fact. I remind myself that everyone else [gets lonely], too. There's someone out there lying in bed with a married partner... and they are both LONELY.

I look at this life as boot camp. I am learning from my problems, and I'm learning to be whole in Christ just as I am. but I also know that nothing—and no one—in this life is going to make me totally happy. I'm not going to find complete happiness until I'm back home, face to face with Jesus.

Susie: *How are you preparing for your future mate?*

Cindy: I don't think we can ever prepare ourselves totally to be in a marriage relationship, because it's foreign to us. I don't believe it's necessary to focus our lives on preparing for marriage.

To me, the focus is, "Lord, with or without someone, I want to walk with you. I want to read my Bible every day. I want to pray with you every day and I want my life to become more whole and complete in you."

Seek first the kingdom of God and his righteousness and all these things will be added unto you. Seek God—not a relationship. When the time comes, God will bring that person into your life. I'm a romantic, so I really believe that.

There have been a couple of relationships in my life where the guy was nice, dressed great, was a Christian, and seemed perfect. But he *wasn't* right because I didn't love him. If we prepare our hearts in God, he'll tell us who he wants us to love.

Carman: I'm not preparing for a mate. I'm doing all I can to be transformed into the image of Jesus. But I *do* believe that compatibility is important in the type of woman I date.

Kirk: I'm making every effort to not be too set in my ways. The older I get, the more I realize what little control I have over my life. The fact is, not one of us has total control. If you don't know the Lord and you're not following God's will, then you're asking for anything to happen to you. You're like a sitting duck for the devil to take pot shots at.

Susie: *Got some tips on how guys and girls can maximize their dating lives?*

Cindy: (Girls, let your guy friends read this!) For the guys, pray first about the girls you date. Then treat them the way you would your mother—with respect and reverence.

Above all, be yourself (don't put on some kind of silly macho act). Be the unique person God made you to be and find a woman who'll be a good friend. A relationship is basically a great friendship.

Pam: Keep Proverbs 4:23 in mind: "Above all else, guard your affections. For they influence everything else in your life." Be careful with your heart and how much of it you give away. Let that trust build gradually. You don't want your heart to get wounded more than it has to.

Ask lots of questions and get to know your partner over a period of time... slowly. Most important of all, make sure your date is worthy of being trusted.

Carman: Remember that if you've blown it in the past—like losing your virginity or having an abortion—God will restore your innocence... if you let him. Go back to him and ask for forgiveness. Ask him to be Lord of your singleness and dating life.

Mark: If you like yourself, then potential dates will like you, too. Do everything you can to improve your body—mentally, physically, and spiritually. For me, that means having solid friends who know the real Mark Lowry—friends I can spill my guts to.

Also, get involved in a Bible study... and while you're at it, exercise your bod. If there's something about yourself that you want to change, then don't just sit back and whine... get busy and do it.

Here's another tip: Learn all you can about the opposite sex. Men don't care if the toothpaste cap is on right. Women do.

Hey, once you've learned a few things, give me a call, OK?

Kirk: When you're thinking about marriage, keep this in mind: Don't date or pursue marriage because of circumstances. Get married because you can't live without that person. Life is difficult enough without having to try to make something work. It should be a natural thing.

Some of you may be skeptical and think, *That just doesn't happen.* Well, I believe it does. I know married couples who've been together for thirty years and they're *still* chasing each other around the house.

Some young singles are in love with the idea of being in love and aren't asking the important question: "Is this going to work in real life?"

Ji: Stay sexually pure. I'm proud to say that I'm a virgin... and I plan to stay that way until marriage. The fact is, sex was designed for marriage. So you're really in dangerous territory if you get into light or heavy petting. Why not "play around" a little? Because it all leads in one direction: sexual intercourse.

If you really believe your relationship is in the will of God, then you can take a lot of preventive measures in keeping sexual purity a part of your life. Here are my suggestions:

1. *Don't pray together.* I know this sounds a little shocking, but here's my reasoning: Prayer is an intimate thing that creates a bond. I think that in God's design, spirituality and sexuality is such an intertwined thing. In today's society, we kind of dissect that into different quarters and say this is this and this is that. I don't believe that. I believe God created us with all these parts that intertwine. The physical thing intertwines with the spiritual thing, and the sexual thing intertwines with everything else.

2. *Even though you may THINK you don't need them, you still need to set boundaries.* Date in groups or try double-dating. Don't be alone for too long, and do all you can to avoid falling into temptation.

As these fun singles have pointed out, dating isn't the most important thing in the world. And being single isn't the worst thing in the world. Determine to enjoy life *right now*—whether you're dating someone or not. If you'll ask God to help you become content and fulfilled, he'll answer your prayer and meet your needs.

Repeat after me: *The most important thing in the world is NOT the opposite sex—it's my relationship with Jesus Christ.*

A FINAL WORD

Hopefully, dating during your teen years will turn out to be one of your fondest memories. I want you to be able to look back ten years from now and smile at the good times you had and the things you learned from your dating relationships.

I don't want you to look back and struggle with regret because of bad choices you made during adolescence. I know God doesn't want that, either.

God wants you to have successful relationships with the opposite sex even more than you do! He wants to help you in establishing great relationships with guys. He wants you to learn many wonderful lessons from the guys you date, as well as the ones who are your friends.

God also wants to be your strength when you face the temptations that young people face in their dating relationships. When the pressure is on and you're feeling the heat, please remember that he's there with you! He will *never* allow any temptation to cross your path that's too big for you to handle. The truth is, he will provide you with everything you need to be successful at maintaining godly relationships.

So during these exciting teen years, try to remember that good choices equal good consequences, and that bad choices equal bad consequences. Determine to make good choices. Ten years from now, I want you to be able to look over your shoulder with GREAT memories!

For a free copy of *Brio*, a magazine for teen girls, write:

Focus on the Family
P.O. Box 35500
Colorado Springs, CO 80935-3550

or call 1-800-232-6459.